EXECUTIVE THINKING

LESLIE L. KOSSOFF

THE DREAM

EXECUTIVE

THE VISION

THINKING

THE MISSION

ACHIEVED

Davies-Black Publishing
Palo Alto, California

Published by Davies-Black Publishing, an imprint of Consulting Psychologists Press, Inc., 3803 East Bayshore Road, Palo Alto, CA 94303; 800-624-1765.

Special discounts on bulk quantities of Davies-Black books are available to corporations, professional associations, and other organizations. For details, contact the Director of Book Sales at Davies-Black Publishing, an imprint of Consulting Psychologists Press, Inc., 3803 East Bayshore Road, Palo Alto, CA 94303; 650-691-9123; Fax 650-623-9271.

Davies-Black web site: www.cpp-db.com

03 02 01 00 99   10 9 8 7 6 5 4 3 2 1

Printed in the United States of America

Library of Congress Cataloging-in-Publication Data

Kossoff, Leslie L.
     Executive thinking : the dream, the vision, the mission
achieved / Leslie L. Kossoff. — 1st ed.
          p. cm.
     ISBN 0-89106-134-7 (hardcover)
     1. Executive ability. 2. Management.   I. Title.
HD38.2.K675 1999
     658.4'09 — dc21   99–23015
                                                                CIP

FIRST EDITION

First printing 1999

Contents

Conviction

PART ONE

DREAMS

ORGANIZATIONS EXIST based on and because of dreams. Dreams of success. Dreams of product or service differentiation. Dreams of creating an enterprise the likes of which have never been known before.

It does not matter whether the organization is a first franchise with the possibility of multiple sites. Neither does it matter if the organization is a long-standing institution moving into its newest evolution. Nor does it matter if it is the brainchild of a new entrepreneur who has never worked in an organization before.

The dreams are the same. They are grand and glorious dreams, bursting with color and light. They are the dreams of executives.

Executives not only see things. They do things. They make things happen. Executives not only dream the dream of the organization, but they take the necessary actions to ensure that the dream becomes reality.

Even in the most frustrating of times, executives don't lose sight of their dream. No matter what the obstacles, executives believe that their dream not only can but will become reality.

If anything, challenge makes executives all the more intent on making their dream reality. These are not amorphous, romantic illusions. They are detailed, exquisite, tangible pictures of what the organization can, should, and will be.

6

Executives are tough. They have to be. It is not easy to dream, let alone to constantly expose one's dream to the reality of a world in constant flux, sometimes seemingly with every odd stacked against success.

Executives hold onto their dream through thick or thin. They find ways to make their dream reality—no matter what the challenges or odds against success. If it is not in this iteration, it will be in another. But it will be. That is the non-negotiable. Their dream will be.

It is just that commitment and intent that make executives executives. It is why their organizations exist and continue to exist. It is why the organization looks to them for guidance, support, and direction. It is why the people who make up the organization look to them for safety and security, betting their lives and livelihoods on the dream and actions of the executive of the organization.

Why Pictures and Dreams Are Important

It has been said that if you don't know where you are going, any road will take you there. Such is the case in an organization without the benefit of the executive's pictures and dream.

In order to succeed—really succeed—an organization must have a clear direction and understanding of where it is going. That direction and understanding resides within the executive. Whether at the most senior level or within the managerial ranks, without the executive-level understanding of the purpose, the true aim of the organization, the organization will never fully achieve its goals.

It will come close. It will achieve many things. It can still be successful. But for the organization to be more, to excel beyond anything previously imagined, the executive's dream is an absolute necessity.

Beyond the organization's needs, there are the executive's needs as well. Executives thrive on the development of the pictures and dream. Everything they look at, everything they do, sparks thoughts about what else might be, what is yet to come.

From that, the executives move even further in their own as well as the organization's development. We are all aware that only those organizations that do not rest on their laurels survive the test of time. In the last quarter of the twentieth century we saw industries that were believed to be inviolate come under attack the likes of which had never been seen before.

Historically, within the United States, it was said "What is good for General Motors is good for the country." In the 1970s, when General Motors, Ford, and Chrysler were under siege by the Japanese automobile industry, the world saw exactly what happens when an organization or an industry rests on its laurels. It was neither good for General Motors nor good for the United States.

It was, however, a wake-up call to executives throughout the world about just how important it is to keep dreaming, to keep striving.

Conversely, during that same period the world also saw the benefits and outcomes of pictures and dreams the likes of which had never been seen before. Upstart companies such as Apple and Microsoft took on industries and organizations to create new worlds.

Some, like Apple, have reinvented themselves many times in the ensuing years. Others, like Microsoft, have become to the world what General Motors had previously been to the United States. In all cases, these executives have created industries and opportunities coming solely from their dream—and their ability to make others see and understand their dream, ultimately leading others to join them in the accomplishment of the dream.

And that, too, is the importance of the dream for the executive. In organizations, with great forethought and planning, dreams do come true.

❦

Vision Versus Vision Statements

There is a very real difference between the pictures and dreams described here and the vision statements most commonly found in organizations. Only by understanding and acting upon that difference can an executive make the most of his vision for the organization.

In order to fully understand the importance of the pictures and the dream that include that vision, a differentiation must be made between vision and vision statements as they have been applied in organizations to date. The easiest way to make the differentiation is to think about the difference between a Vision *For* the organization and a Vision *Of* the organization.

Executive Thinking is based on a Vision *For* the organization. It is an active vision, one that does not stand idly by as an impossible dream. It is a real and tangible direction with look and feel attached to it. It is action oriented, strategically based, and task supported.

That Vision For the organization includes everybody in the organization as well as all those who support it. It is a vision of universal success, open-ended promise, and ongoing striving for more. Everybody has a part and everybody plays that part. Each sees the benefit and results of her participation. No one and nothing is passive.

A Vision For the organization is accomplished every day in every action taken. Achievement is constant and continuous, always building to the greater goals and the greater good of the organization. Those goals, too, actively build every day with every action taken.

In the case of a vision-oriented organization built on the executive's pictures and dream, the organization is in a constant state of success and achievement, with each person knowing that he or she has added to that achievement by his or her actions. Rather than waiting to achieve some far-flung success, that success is always at hand and always being refined, developed, and built upon.

Vision For the organization is an active voice in the present and everlastingly future tenses.

In contrast, a Vision *Of* the organization is passive. It is seen but not real to the executive or his organization. It does not include specific action toward the organization's goals. It is a static picture of some organization sometime in the future.

A Vision Of the organization looks to the future to include the achievement of the organization's goals, but it does not include the accomplishment of those goals in the immediate actions of the organization and its people.

A Vision Of the organization is a passive voice in the future tense alone.

It is sad but true that this passive version of vision has become the way by which most organizations view this vital component. Vision statements have been made part of the organizational hyperbole in the last few decades. We are told that we must have vision statements to lead our organizations. And we do. We have vision statements. They don't do much in most cases, but we have them.

Vision statements may have started as the pictures and dream of the executive. However, somewhere along the way, in becoming vision statements, they were turned into near advertising slogans for the organization.

"We will be the premier provider of . . . in our industry."

"We will be the best and the most innovative in our industry."

"We will offer the most value to our shareholders, customers, and employees in our industry."

"We will be the largest and most successful company in (our industry, the world, the universe)."

One might scoff at these statements as being bad examples of what vision consists of. However, these vision statements, or versions thereof, are in fact common to many organizations' direction when they first sit down to determine where they are going.

Vision statements, designed to be always slightly unattainable, were to be used by the organization as a direction and a guide. Supported by the organization's mission and values, it was the intent of these statements to create and provide an exciting world of potential to the employees of the organization.

Unfortunately, the value of the vision was lost in the process. As well, the results did not bear out the expectations of the vision when it was being written.

What happened? Where did it go wrong?

The first and biggest problem is that the creation of the vision statement was treated as a task by most organizations. Someone, somewhere, whether in a book or an article, from a consultant, or from a member of the organization, convinced the executive that it was necessary to have a vision statement for the organization to survive and thrive. This moved the process away from being one of ongoing thinking and action to one consisting of a specific task to be accomplished and completed, and then moving on to whatever task was next. Worse, what came next might or might not have had anything to do with the vision statement just created. Usually it did not.

Second, the vision, rather than being presented as the beautiful, Technicolor pictures and dream of the executive, was presented as an advertising slogan. It was expected that, from this sound bite, the organization would understand where it was going and how each person's actions would assist in getting it there. This is unrealistic and unfair to the executive as well as to the organization.

Third, the vision statement was often developed by a committee. This, in and of itself, should not be a problem. However, it may very well become a problem if that committee is working to develop the statement before the pictures have had a chance to gain breadth and depth in the executive's mind.

The executive must be able to speak to his vision clearly and charismatically in order for others to know where it is that he sees the organization going and why. That clear, exciting picture is the one that must be communicated, translated, and demonstrated to the rest of the organization through the actions and words of the executive and his executive and management staff.

If the vision statement is presented to the body of the organization prior to that time, we are left with the situations and scenarios so common to organizations today. Executives, managers, and employees alike skeptically view vision as organizational pretty words. Lots of form, no substance.

Again, this is the sad but true outcome of implementation without forethought. The intent was noble. The method was madness.

Vision For the organization, that action-oriented, present- and future-based view, based on the pictures and dream of the executive, is the direction and method that must be taken. Only by doing so will the executive and the organization be assured of real, long-lasting, and overwhelming success.

ℰⓄℒ

Where the Dream Comes From

Whether executives realize it or not, they operate to their dream based on the pictures in their heads. These are not pictures of specific shareholder value or profit margins. Nor are they necessarily pictures of particular products or services.

These are the pictures of an organization that separates itself from the rest. This organization provides a product or service that is of value to and valued by the marketplace. The organization operates in such a way that every stakeholder—from suppliers to employees to customers and shareholders—is happy to do business with the enterprise.

These are the pictures of an organization directed and operated in the image of the executive. One that knows, understands, and operates to her dream. It is an organization that shares that dream and works as actively as the executive to ensure that the dream comes true.

Usually the pictures are unformed. Rarely do executives give themselves the time to fully develop their pictures. Too often the immediate needs of the organization preclude the executive spending time in her head, with her pictures, developing her dream. Quite often the success of the enterprise itself causes the executive to forget that the success occurred because of her dream and that, without continuing to develop that dream, the organization risks losing its position in the marketplace.

The executive, in order to fulfill her own potential and the potential of the organization, must operate to the expectation that this type of thinking is an organizational norm. That the development of such pictures throughout the organization, on all levels and in all functions, is an expected part of every employee's job. And, more than anything, that that norm is most fully demonstrated by the executive herself.

The pictures in the executive's head, no matter how fully or not fully formed, are iterative and evolutionary. The dream does not rest on laurels. The executive is continually thinking about what else, what more, and why not.

But where does the dream come from? And how does the executive know that it is there?

Sometimes the dream comes from previous experiences, both good and bad. Keep in mind, executives not only see things, they do things. They take action. This occurs even before they have the power base to affect and influence the whole of the organization. In the interim, they take their knowledge and experience and apply them to their enterprise. These early thoughts and actions make up a part of the dream.

Other parts of the dream come from observation. Whether in the work setting or in their private lives, executives store up information for later application. They may forget the specific details of what they saw and where they saw it. However, they do not forget the importance of the message gained. Ultimately, again, they apply these observations to the enterprise.

Finally, because dreaming is a creative process, the pictures and dream simply come from within the executive. This is the part of the process that is hardest to describe yet most crucial to the overall sense of success and accomplishment for the executive herself as well as for the organization she serves.

Executives don't want to copy what others do. They want to create for themselves. They want to learn from others but build their own vision of what is and what can be. They are leaders in the truest sense of the word. They are trailblazers and pioneers, venturing into previously unknown and sometimes uncharted territories, knowing only that they will discover and achieve more than anyone ever has before.

The executive must give herself time to access and describe those pictures. She must force herself to step away from her tasks, whether for seconds, minutes, or hours, and simply look within to discover that which has never been seen before. Once she does so, the formation of the pictures, dream, and Vision For the organization will begin. Ultimately, by continuing the process, the dream will be realized and exceeded over and over again.

Dreams, Pictures, and Executive Thinking

Without the dream, there is no Executive Thinking. It is both that simple and that profound.

The executive's dream and pictures are the basis for the excellence the organization will achieve. That excellence will come from everyone thinking and seeing what it is the executive has dreamed and communicated.

This is not to say that without pursuing this process the organization will fail. It will not. It can still succeed, but only to a certain, measurable extent.

To create an organization that exceeds all that has been seen before, in product, service, satisfaction, and profit, it takes more than just conventional thinking. It takes more than what has been seen up until now. It takes Executive Thinking based on the dream, pictures, and vision of the executive himself.

More important, for the executive to fulfill his known potential and exceed even his own dream of accomplishment, it is imperative that he give himself permission to dream. No one can put limitations on another person's thoughts. That means that it is the executive who stops himself from going beyond. It is the executive who either forces himself into the conventional stream or grabs his life and the life of his organization with both hands and creates a new future.

It is that excitement, that sense of possibility, that forms the basis of Executive Thinking for the executive and the organization. It is that vision, and the belief that the vision can be achieved, that ultimately leads the organization into previously unknown success. It is that belief, coming from the depths of the executive, that leads the members of the organization to ally themselves with the dream, to become a part of it, to believe that they, too, can and will achieve more than ever before.

Executive Thinking is not conventional thinking, nor is it a conventional organizational process. It is one in which, based on the dream of the executive, everyone becomes involved as an active participant in the shared dream. It is both tangible and amorphous. It is both process and result. It is the life and breath of the organization.

༄༅༅

Forming the Dream—the Ground Rules

The actual formation of the dream is an understandable, stepwise process. There are, however, some ground rules that must be laid prior to beginning the process. These ground rules are initially both conscious and inviolate. Eventually, as the executive builds her dreaming technique and comfort level, she may well find that the rules have become an unconscious part of her thinking process and that violations can occur—but only for good cause.

The first ground rule is that there are no wrong answers. No matter where the executive's thinking might lead, there is no reason to believe from the outset that what is thought cannot be achieved. The whole purpose of forming the dream is to go beyond the conventional. That means that conventional wisdom will tell the executive that her dream is an impossibility. This is simply not true—at least not over the long term.

The second ground rule is to suspend disbelief. It is both easy and usually unconscious to put obstacles in the way of progress. Most often, those obstacles come from disbelief in either the executive's own or her organization's ability to achieve what has been dreamed. And so it is important to suspend disbelief. The executive must think, from the outset, that what she has envisioned can and will, in fact, be achieved. She must believe in her own dream as well as in her ability to make that dream come true.

The third and fourth ground rules are preparatory for when the dreaming process has begun. It is at this point, while the dream is being developed or is first being exposed to others, that the executive and her dream can be most vulnerable. It is at this point that the executive, having gotten past her own self-imposed obstacles, risks taking her thoughts, her dream, to a trusted public— those with whom she works most closely. Ground rules three and four prepare and protect the executive for and from that initial process of exposure and its potential outcomes.

The third ground rule is for the executive to monitor her behavior in the early stages of the dreaming process. Dreaming is seductive. Once the executive allows herself to really give way to her thoughts, she will want to tell people. She will want to immediately share her vision. She will want everyone to see what she sees. The problem is that at that point, no one else can, does, or possibly should see what the executive sees.

Remember that the executive has saved up all of her pictures for a long time. Once she gives herself permission to let her mind go, access the pictures, and develop her vision, she will, understandably, want everyone to know and join in. The problem is that, if it is too early, neither she nor the organization will be quite ready. As well, it is important for the executive to realize that, the beauty of her dream notwithstanding, most people will want to poke holes in the dream before entertaining the idea of accepting it.

It is perfectly permissible for the executive to question and probe others about the dream even in its early stages. This will give further breadth and depth to the dream. However, this should be done in very broad terms. The questions should be "What do you think about?" questions. They should not be detailed, nor should they be dream specific. They should be industry and organization oriented. It is then up to the executive to determine how, why, and whether the answers have any bearing upon her dream.

The executive should not seem as if she is keeping secrets from those around her. The questioning and probing may be a different behavior from those demonstrated before. The distraction of the thinking process may also be perceived as a change in behavior. While the executive doesn't want to give the game away prematurely (keep in mind, others are probably not working to the first two ground rules), she also does not want to cause undue concern in the organization. And change leads to concern.

By monitoring her behavior and by observing the behavior of others, the executive will be laying the appropriate groundwork for successful implementation once the thinking begins to be expanded to include the rest of the organization. This will ultimately build added support for the dream and allay the concerns that normally come with any change.

The fourth ground rule, and sometimes a real stumbling block, is to separate the dream from the individual. Dreaming and the dream that results are a very personal process and outcome. This is the dream of the individual who dreams it. This is the dream of the executive.

The executive must understand that, until others see what she sees, the dream may seem delusional to those who initially see and hear it. This is neither a commentary on the dream nor about the individual who dreamed it. It is a natural and normal reaction to everything from being presented with the unexpected (remember ground rules one and two) to realizing that nothing will ever be quite the same again.

The executive has been dreaming her dream, whether consciously or unconsciously, for a long time. To the executive, the dream is real and can be achieved. To those who are first exposed to the dream, it is new, different, and frightening. It will change their lives.

No one, upon being exposed to a new thought or experience, is ever the same as before. They are changed. They know something they didn't know before. Whether or not they choose to adopt and act upon that idea or experience, it has been incorporated into their lives.

Executive dreams are big, beautiful, and challenging. They are life and world changing. They create dreams in others.

This can lead to real fear in those who are hearing the dream. "What if the dream works? What if it doesn't? What will the impact be on me? Will it be for the good or the bad? Can I trust this person who has dreamed this dream?"

The executive must understand that her dream will eventually become the dream of the organization and all those who share in its process, prosperity, and success. By not taking the reactions of the hearers personally, the executive will keep her thinking, and her ability to observe the thinking of others, clear and objective. This will lead the way to a full and successful implementation of Executive Thinking and, ultimately, to the original dream and its ongoing iterations coming true.

ℒ⊚ℒ

Forming the Dream—the Process

The process of forming the dream is one of questions and answers. These questions and answers are both asked and answered by the executive himself. Even when the questions or answers are externally based, the executive must reach inside himself for his truth and his understanding of what it is he is seeing.

Dreaming is a visceral process. It is one of gut feeling, instinct, and internal belief systems. It is not sweet and romantic. Neither is it particularly chivalrous. The dream may be big and beautiful, but it takes no prisoners. It is a hard-line, action-oriented direction for the organization— where it is going, and where it will go when it passes its initial goals.

It is crucial that the executive reach within himself to truly ask—and answer—the questions "What does *my* organization look like? How does it feel to work there? For me? For others? What do I want to achieve? How will I know when I have achieved it?"

And, from there, "When I have, what's next? Once I have accomplished what I have set out to do (because I will) what comes next? What constitutes *my* ever-growing, ever-developing enterprise—the one that goes far beyond anything seen before?"

This is the internal assessment and dreaming process. It is the one that puts no limits on product or service, market or market share. It is the most global, yet in many ways the most defining, aspect of the dream. It is, exquisitely and exclusively, the executive's dream.

From that point, the questions and answers access previous knowledge and experience. "What have I learned from this organization? From others? How does this organization really work? How would I like it to work? What would I like others to say about this organization once it has begun fulfilling my dream? What strength do I bring to the organization that I will use and build upon to assist in fulfilling the dream?"

These are initial defining questions. They are personal, yet they are externally based. They are global, although at this point the executive may find himself focusing in on product or service. They are no longer exclusively about the executive's personal dream. They are now about the dream in the context of the organization.

If the organization does not yet exist, these questions can still be asked. In many cases, entrepreneurs find themselves ousted from their brainchild organization because they focused so exclusively on product or service that they forgot to dream about the organization and prepare for its growth. By asking these questions from the outset, the executive—even of a one-person organization—prepares himself for the explosive growth that will come with the organization's success.

The next set of questions is observational. In these questions, the executive looks to and at other resources as a guide to further defining his dream. "Which organizations do I hold in high esteem? Why? For which organizations do I have little respect? Why? Whom do I or would I like to consider my role model among executives in other firms? In my own? What is it he or she brings to the organization that I would like to emulate?"

In asking and answering these questions, the executive begins a comparative assessment as part of the development of his dream. While the dream is new and different, it is important for the executive to include as part of the dream his knowledge, experience, and observations of other organizations' operations. This assists in the initial preparation of the dream and its fulfillment for the marketplace.

Once the executive has begun the dreaming process by asking these questions, he must prepare for the time when the dream goes public. The executive must realize that, because his dream is iterative and evolutionary, there will never be a time when it is finished. The dream will go public while it is still a developmental entity. As it begins to be applied within the organization and viewed initially, exclusively, by others in the executive team, the dream will take on further depth, breadth, and organizational applicability and understanding.

Finally, it is important to note that, with the exception of two questions in the observational set, all of the questions are to the positive. This makes the dream formation process far more difficult than one would expect. For the most part, we are trained to look to what we have not done, what cannot be or has not yet been accomplished. We rarely congratulate ourselves on our accomplishments. Indeed, we take our accomplishments for granted.

This is a grave mistake. In order for the executive to be able to fully dream, he must first create a safety net for himself and his dream. He must acknowledge and congratulate himself on what he has accomplished thus far. This will allow him to understand that, in fact, the dream can be accomplished. After all, look at what he has already done. There is no reason why the newer, bigger, more fully defined dream cannot also come true.

One of the hallmarks of executives as a group is that they are pragmatic dreamers. They know what they want to accomplish, and they know the existing limitations that might present obstacles. Those obstacles don't stop the executives. The executives know that they will simply have to think harder to work their way around, over, under, or through whatever gets in their way. No matter what, the obstacles won't stop them.

Dreams are positive. Executives are positive as well. Executive Thinking, based on the dream of the executive, is the intentional application of positive direction and action for the organization, in which everyone knows where she is going, why, how the organization is going to get there, and what part she will play in the achievement of that goal.

The pictures, dream, and vision of the executive provide the basis of that direction. They are the necessary foundation upon which the rest of the organization's success will be built.

E X E C U T I V E   T H O U G H T S

Executives not only see things. They do things. They make things happen. Executives not only dream the dream of the organization, but they take the actions to ensure that the dream becomes reality.

Executive dreams are big, beautiful, and challenging. They are life and world changing. They create dreams in others. To the executive, the dream is real and can be achieved. To those who are exposed to the dream, it is new, different, and frightening. It will change their lives.

The executive must realize that, because his dream is iterative and evolutionary, there will never be a time when it is finished.

CHAPTER 2

ROLE

THE IMPACT
and results of Executive Thinking are universal. The executive, the organization, customers, suppliers, and shareholders all benefit. The role of the executive in Executive Thinking, however, is internal. Rather than seeing herself from the perspective of the marketplace, in order to make Executive Thinking succeed the executive must understand her role in the eyes of the organization itself.

The Psychological Impact of the Executive on the Organization

In a speech to members of the National Press Club, author Tom Clancy, in answering questions, spoke of two aspects of war: the physical and the psychological. In differentiating the two, he explained that human life, its threat and loss, constituted the physical aspects of war. The psychological aspect of war as he described it was based in great part on the belief the soldiers and their country had in their leader.

Clancy explained that the greatest threat in war is that a seed of doubt might be planted in the minds of the country's defenders, whether soldiers or citizens. That is why, he posited, removing the country's leader from his position during a time of war is absolutely devastating and can cause the country to lose its fight.

This same logic applies to the executive—not so much to draw the comparison of business and war, but to understand the role and the impact of the executive on her organization. Executives are the leaders of the organization. They give the organization its purpose and direction. If they believe in the organization and what it is doing, so, too, will those who make up the body of the organization. The better the executive clearly and consistently presents that purpose and direction, the more the management and employees will act accordingly.

The level of importance the organization places on its executive is enormous. Employees look to their executive for assurance that the organization is moving in the

28

right direction. In part, this is because they want to feel that the work they are providing has value. More important, they want to be assured that the executive, who from their perspective holds their livelihood in her hands, is moving the organization in the right direction to ensure and improve upon that livelihood over time.

Employees want to trust their executive. They want to believe that the executive has their best interest at heart, as if the executive knows them personally. They want to feel a collaboration with their executive in achieving the executive's, the organization's, and their own goals. They want to feel and be a part of the dream of the executive.

This gives the executive a great advantage in achieving her goals for the organization. Because the employees begin by wanting to trust and believe in their executive, the executive begins with the win on her side. It is only when the organization either does not understand or does not know what it is the executive is thinking or doing that that trust and belief becomes shaken within the organization. At that point, the advantage to the executive is lost.

As with Clancy's explanation, there can be no room for the seed of doubt to be placed within the minds of the people who make up the organization. There must be a clear understanding and acceptance of what it is the executive wants and intends to achieve. There must be a shared vision: a clear view and understanding of the pictures and dream in the executive's head.

This, too, is the basis of Executive Thinking. By understanding her psychological importance to her organization, the executive is in a position to build upon the shared dreams of others toward achieving her and the organization's goals. These combined dreams utilize the best of what each individual has to offer—all applied toward the greater good.

The executive can and must build on her psychological advantage in the organization not only to communicate and promote her dream, but also to explain and access how the shared dream can only work to the organization's best interests. This will not only allow the expansion of the executive's dream, it will also begin the reciprocal trust-building process that is crucial to Executive Thinking and to the long-term success of the organization.

To a great extent, executives themselves are not aware or conscious of their psychological importance to and impact on the organization. Because the executive is focusing on her tasks and responsibilities, she is unaware that, from the perspective of her employees, it is she who makes the organization make sense or not. It is she who creates the foundation for the trust the employees have in the organization.

℘◉℘

Executives, Perceptions, and Organizational Actions

Executives would probably be appalled if they knew how much time their employees spend discussing them. Pieces of personal information, perceptions about the executive's beliefs, discussions about the executive's history, and more are given airtime among employees.

Employees want to feel a sense of kinship with their executive. They want to believe that their executive knows and believes in them, and that they are more than just a number in some departmental or organizational summary. Employees look for acknowledgment by and also ways of acknowledging their executive. It is, simultaneously and paradoxically, both a distant and a close relationship.

Employees act based on what they believe their executive wants from them. If it is speed at the cost of quality, they will focus on schedule. If it is quality no matter at what cost, they will focus on product or service quality. They may never be given this or any other specific direction in this regard. It doesn't matter. The employees truly do want to do what they believe their executive wants.

Although it is out of favor to think so, the relationship between employees and their executive is and will remain parental. This is a function of a hierarchical structure, no matter how many layers there may or may not be.

Employees look to their executive for direction. Executives direct their employees. Employees look to their executive to provide guidelines and limitations. Executives provide exactly that in the form of everything from vision to policy and procedures.

It is not that the employees are unthinking lemmings running this way and that with no thoughts of their own. On the contrary, employees are great thinkers. They think about what's wrong. They think about what they can and can't do—or believe they can and can't do. They think about what they would like to be different—including the ways by which they receive guidance from and provide feedback to their executive.

They think about their executive and the organization as it exists. Often, they blame the executive for the state of the organization, not knowing that neither does the organization have to be that way, nor does the executive want it that way. Based on their uninformed perspective, the employees think the organization has to be the way it is because the executive either isn't paying attention, is working her own agenda, or simply doesn't know better. Worse yet, they take action on their uninformed thinking, often unintentionally hurting the organization in the process.

While the executive is asking, "Why doesn't this organization work the way it should and the way I thought it would?" the employees are thinking, "If only the executive would pay attention to the things that count, we could do what she keeps saying she wants us to do." This organizational breakdown exists exactly because of the discrepancies and inconsistencies in thinking. This most frequently found organizational norm is the exact opposite of Executive Thinking.

℘☉℘

The Organization as a Reflection of Its Executive

Knowingly or not, executives form their organizations in their own image. This is both good and to be expected. After all, the organization is the outgrowth of the executive himself: his dream and vision, his actions in getting to where he is, and his beliefs about himself and his organization.

The importance for the executive is to realize that, consciously or not, the organization adopts what it believes to be that image. Whatever it is that the employees see, perceive, or believe about their executive will be reflected within the body of the organization.

No matter how complex the structure, no matter how many locations domestically and internationally, no matter how many products or services provided, the organization is a reflection of its executive. That image is pervasive in both the thinking and the actions of the management and employees at all levels. In most cases, without ever trying, the executive has created a perspective and a mind-set that form the basis of how the organization operates.

If the executive is perceived to be driven, so, too, will the organization be driven. If the executive is quiet and soft-spoken, so, too, will the organization behave in that way. In neither case does it necessarily mean that the organization will succeed or fail. It simply means that the organization follows suit from what it sees, perceives, and believes of its executive.

As noted before, this is a clear advantage for the executive. Executives can and must give their organizations a sense of purpose. No matter how small or large the organization, as long as the executive projects and portrays an understanding of where he and the organization are going and why, the body of the organization will follow suit.

It can be argued that this is simply organizational "spin." It is not. No matter whether employees are working in a job to keep the bills paid or in a career with an eye toward a grander and more glorious future, they want to know that they have allied themselves with an organization that will get them there. It is the executive to whom they look to determine whether or not that will be the case.

This puts a particular onus on the executive to be aware of the image he is projecting and to understand that the organization is looking to him to determine the image and actions they must project. Again and always, employees look to their executive for guidance. This is one of the ways not only by which employees do so, but also that gives them greatest satisfaction. If they are working, as they believe, in the image and toward the goals of their executive, then they are working to the benefit of the organization. They are also satisfying something in themselves and, so they believe, in their executive for which they will ultimately be recognized and rewarded.

It is important, too, for executives to remember that the most valuable forms of recognition and reward are not necessarily monetary. In most cases, trust and loyalty—in effect the relationship to and with the organization—are viewed as being far more important than monetary reward.

By acting in the perceived image of their executive, employees feel themselves rewarded just by virtue of their doing the right thing. They are acting in the appropriate manner and toward what they believe to be the greater good. They believe that they are acting as their executive wants them to act. Ultimately, this will result in monetary reward, whether in the form of salary increases, bonuses or profit sharing, increased stock value, or simply safe and continued employment. The monetary reward is not the driver. It is the expected result.

The driver is the desire of the employees to be a part of something of value. What is considered of value, however, is that which is interpreted by the employees as being of value to their executive. Whether they get it right or not is up to the executive himself—the extent to which he communicates his values and goals and the purpose and intent of the organization.

Once again, the executive must look at his psychological impact on the organization. As the leader he is looked to not only for the guidance and direction required but also as the first and greatest safety net in the organization. Management and employees alike put their trust in their executive to know that his way is the right way not only for the organization but also for each individual the organization houses.

ᏨᎧᏒ

Executives and the Parallel Universe

Executives live and work in parallel universes. One universe, the one with which they are most familiar, is the one in which they are making ongoing difficult and strategic decisions. It is the world of profit and loss, of shareholder value, and, in many cases, of media and public perceptions.

This primary universe exists for the executive whether she is most senior in her organization or a member of the executive or management staff. For those most senior, the public perceptions about which she is concerned often come from shareholders, brokers, fund managers, and analysts. For those who hold less than the most senior position, the public perception of concern is often from the board, executive staff members, the next potential employer, or the industry as a whole.

In both cases, these are external perspectives. While they must be taken into consideration, they drive the actions of the executive in directions that may not be preferred but are deemed to be necessary. This contrasts directly with the understanding the executive has gained of the importance of the pictures in her head, her dream and vision.

Just as in the case of the executive's internal development of the direction of the organization, in understanding her role she must, once again, look within. But this time, in looking within, she is looking within the body of the organization that she oversees and for which she is responsible.

The secondary universe, the one that she understands is there but doesn't live in as actively and continuously, is the universe of the executive's impact on the employees and the body of the organization. This is the universe in which Executive Thinking resides once implemented. This is the universe in which the executive's ability to achieve all that she has set out to achieve either comes to fruition or does not.

This secondary universe is one that the executive leaves as she moves up the corporate ladder and pursues her dream and her career. As she leaves this secondary universe farther and farther behind, her focus on and understanding of the impact of the executive on that universe diminishes. She has learned how to think like an executive and she has been rewarded for it. She now lives in the primary universe of the executive—that externally driven, outwardly perceived universe.

While the executive must never lose sight of that universe and its importance, the only way she will achieve her dream is by actively guiding and directing the secondary universe. This is accomplished through Executive Thinking.

In order to fully and successfully implement Executive Thinking and incorporate it into the organization's operations, the executive must reacquaint herself with the universe of executive impact on the employees. By doing so, the executive positions herself to achieve her dream through understanding how to get other people to see what she sees, make that dream their own, and act accordingly.

ༀ

Executive Impact on the Employee— the Secondary Universe

By the time an executive becomes an executive, he has been out of the employee ranks for quite a while. His thoughts have been focused not only on the good of the organization, but also on how the actions he chooses to take or not take will affect his career growth and potential. Executives have plans for themselves as well as for the organization.

Even entrepreneurs just out of college and new to the organizational realm are removed from the ranks of the employees. Their thinking has been product or service based. They have had plans for what they would bring to the marketplace, how it differs from what is already there, and how they, too, can be a Fred Smith, Bill Gates, Anita Roddick, Steve Jobs, or Michael Dell.

No matter what the situation or scenario, the executive has not thought like an employee for a long time. Executives think like executives. They plan. They create. They see things that don't currently exist and they *make* them exist. Executives don't languish. They do things.

Employees do things, too. And when employees don't think like executives, they sometimes do things that don't work to the benefit of the organization. Worse yet, sometimes they do take actions that benefit the organization—only nobody else knows about it.

The first challenge for the executive in establishing Executive Thinking as the norm of the organization is to understand the role of the executive through his own eyes and also through the eyes of his employees. That removal from the standard organizational realm that comes with success eventually comes back to haunt the executive and the organization. The executive must take action to ensure that in everyone's understanding of his goals and vision for the organization, there is no reason or basis for unintentional attack by uninformed employees.

As noted before, executives shouldn't be surprised by how their organization operates—whether that be to the good or to the bad from their perspective. After all, the organization looks just like them, or at least like what the organization perceives as the image of the executive.

This provides both opportunity and challenge to the executive. The opportunity lies in the executive's ability to shift, mold, and change the direction and tone of the organization by understanding his role in the larger context. The challenge is in the amount of time and effort that must go into thinking and strategizing to ensure that the organization's potential is met and exceeded based on that executive's actions and communicated real beliefs.

ౝ౸

ᴀ *Historical Context*

In order to fully understand the impact of the executive on the organization, it is useful to look back at that impact when the executive wasn't even aware that he was having one. And the easiest way to do that is to look at what happened in organizations and their operations during the 1970s, 1980s, and early 1990s when the world of business was changing toward what it must be for the twenty-first century.

Frequently, employees took their cues from the background of the executive at the top of the organization, almost solely depending upon the specialization from which the executive came. Management and employees, even without specific direction, would adjust their actions and decision-making criteria to suit what they believed the focus and direction of the executive to be.

39

If the senior executive came from an engineering background, for example, the assumption was that all budget would go to the research and development (R&D) and engineering design departments. Administration, manufacturing, sales, marketing, and other departments would immediately assume that they were to be underfunded and would act accordingly. Management and employees would begin to complain. Employees would believe—and often erroneously be told by their immediate management—that they couldn't do things that they had done in the past because now the company was engineering driven.

Productivity would decrease simply because the employees believed that they would not be allowed to accomplish their goals no matter what they did. Without ever saying anything, the body of the organization would react as if dicta had been decreed and were being enforced. In fact, in the vast majority of cases, no such dicta were ever decreed.

Should the senior executive position change hands, which it often did, to someone from marketing, the organization would immediately regroup. This was a logical change from the perspective of the employees. From an uninformed, internal perspective it was believed that engineering had probably been designing to their hearts' content—without necessarily designing products that were salable. The focus needed to shift, according to this thinking, to marketing to make sure that the company was pointed in the right direction and had products that would sell.

Internally, the assumption now became that whatever funding had been provided to R&D and engineering design would be pulled, so whatever projects were in the pipeline might as well be forgotten. Everyone else who had been complaining before continued to complain. The new assumption was that sales and marketing were having all the fun: sales trips to premier golf locations, corporate gifts, unending budgets—the good life.

But the time would come and, once again, that senior position would change hands. Now it might go to someone from finance. Once again, this was a logical step for the organization as perceived by the employees. In this case, the uninformed understanding was that marketing was spending too much money without enough return. Thus, it was now necessary for the company to shift focus toward its financial health and well-being.

This ongoing cycle played itself out in countless organizations in the manufacturing and service and public and private sectors. Interestingly, even when the most senior executive did not change, if there were changes in the ranks of the executive staff, or in the beliefs of employees about what was happening in the marketplace, the same assumptions would be made and their associated actions taken by the employees.

In any of these cases, had there been a system of Executive Thinking in place, the organization would have been able to move ahead smartly and without undue difficulty. Employees would have understood at any point what it was that the organization was trying to accomplish. That understanding would have been affected by the change in management. However, the slowdowns and stoppages that organizations experienced would not have occurred.

Instead, because the perception of direction was left to the employees to determine on their own, organizations proceeded in fits and starts. Products did not come to market, quality suffered, and ultimately layoffs were required.

With Executive Thinking implemented within the organization, not only are management and employees better able to adjust to organizational changes, they are positioned to assist the new executive and the organization in its transition and success. Once started, Executive Thinking benefits each and every employee, manager, and executive in the organization—whether currently in residence or not.

The Role of the Executive and Executive Thinking

The executive, her role, and Executive Thinking are inextricably bound. Given that the organization is a reflection of its executive and that the managers and employees of that organization want nothing more than to accomplish what it is the executive wants, it is simply a matter of creating alignment between the two.

Executive Thinking is a reflection of the beliefs about and direction of the organization as viewed by its executive. The executive first commits by communicating her dream and then manifesting her belief in the members of the organization by gaining their thoughts and participation. The executive is the ultimate Executive

Thinker. She knows and understands the power of vision and the even greater power of shared vision.

She knows where she wants to go and how the organization is going to look, feel, and act once it gets there. She is unafraid. She understands that discourse and dialogue are vastly different from adversity and sabotage. She actively participates in and provides support for the first. She is vigilant in her intolerance of the second.

By utilizing her position and the belief in her and her position within the organization, the executive ensures that everyone not only sees what she sees but understands its importance to her, to each individual, and to the organization as a whole. She uses her psychological position and advantage in the organization as a means of gaining and keeping support and understanding throughout the organization.

The executive understands that the organization and **43** its employees have minds of their own. She understands the value and power of those minds—and what those thoughts and actions combined can do to assist her in achieving her goal.

She understands that, whether from her organization or another, each individual housed within the organization has a history of perceptions, beliefs, expectations, and disappointments gained from other experiences. Using her ability to communicate and her understanding of the employees' needs, she gains even further support by engaging the body of the organization in achieving what she seeks. In so doing, she makes her goals and dream the goals and dream of each and every individual in the organization.

The executive does not remove herself from the organization's view. She understands that her focus cannot be so completely on the future and the continual building of the organization that she does not pay adequate attention to the organization as it stands today. Instead, the executive moves comfortably between the two universes to ensure that the direction the organization is going is the one she wants and is reflected by the actions of the people who are taking it there.

Executives look for the discrepancies in the organization with the aid of their associates. In so doing, they engage to determine what actions need to be taken to address those discrepancies, take the actions, and then monitor the results. The executive knows that if a discrepancy between intent and action exists in one segment of the organization, it exists in others as well.

The executive is a vigilant person. Executive Thinking is a vigilant process. It forces the executive to look at her role in the context of the body of the organization. It requires ongoing assessment, analysis, and modification of what is being communicated and how. It develops trust within and between all sectors and levels of the organization. This trust is a direct outcome of the belief in the executive and her vigilance in overseeing all of the needs of the organization—those of its employees included.

Executive Thinking is the human and organizational manifestation of the executive's dream, goals, and vision. It is the ultimate reflection of the executive herself, of a person committed to her accomplishments knowing that not only she but everyone will benefit.

Knowingly or not, executives form their organization in their own image. The importance for the executive is to realize that the organization adopts what it believes to be that image. This puts a particular onus on the executive to be aware of the image he is projecting and to understand that the members of the organization are looking to him to determine the image and actions they must project.

Executives live and work in parallel universes. One universe is the one in which they are making ongoing difficult and strategic decisions. This is an externally oriented universe. The secondary universe is the universe of the executive's impact on the employees and the body of the organization. This is the universe in which Executive Thinking resides.

Executive Thinking is the human and organizational manifestation of the executive's dream, goals, and vision. It is the ultimate reflection of the executive himself, of a person committed to his accomplishments knowing that not only he but everyone will benefit.

45

CHAPTER 3

EXPANSION

BEING AN EXECUTIVE CAN BE lonely. Ultimately it is the executive who is responsible for all of the decisions made—whether they are made directly by him or not. It is the executive who is looked to both in praise and in blame for the organization's success, failure, products, services, operations, image, and everything else.

People situated hierarchically below the executive are looking toward gaining that job themselves. Even when there is trust among associates, the executive is aware that his is the prime position, the goal, the ultimate attainment.

People who are not executives don't understand what it is to be an executive. They tend to mistake its trappings for the job. Mahogany Row. Stock Options. Private Jets. Big Salary.

Rarely do those who do not hold executive positions think about the pressures attached to being an executive. Whether internally or externally, the executive is always under scrutiny. He is both alone and exposed in his actions. The higher up in the organization, the more alone and exposed he becomes.

Still, those within the ranks of the organization look to the executive and his position as a goal. They act in accordance with a dual agenda. The first agenda is usually a personal one — to rise within the organization until such time that their personal career goals are met. The second is to use the organization and its opportunities as a means of achieving their first goal.

One executive described his experience upon becoming CEO as being particularly eye opening in this regard. On having achieved his goal of becoming CEO he realized that, on average, he had been spending about half his time working toward that goal and half his time working on the job at hand. Suddenly, as CEO, he found that he had far more time for the job than previously was the case. He had achieved his objective. Now he could focus on the work that needed to be done.

What, then, were his people doing? Were they following his unconscious example and spending half their time focusing on personal agendas and not on the good of the organization? His frustration was in knowing that if he had been doing that, so, too, were current members of his staff. How, he wondered, could he get them to focus on their job rather than his? What could he do to engage them as part of the organization, knowing that they would be rewarded and recognized for their actions?

What could he do to make them not act in the same way that he had?

This dilemma is at the core of the challenge for the executive, but it also presents his greatest advantage and opportunity. By understanding and working with the dual agendas of his people, the executive can utilize Executive Thinking to achieve his own, the organization's, and each individual's goals all at the same time.

ℰ☉ℰ

Making the Dual Agenda Work for the Organization

One of the purposes and outgrowths of Executive Thinking is to create a single side on which all the employees of the organization stand. This is far more necessary and complex a concept or a possibility than is usually understood.

In most cases, executives, management, and employees alike assume that everyone is working toward the same end. Clearly this is not the case. Even at the individual level a dual agenda exists. Expand that to include the rest of the organization and the agendas being simultaneously played out both personally and organizationally are innumerable.

The dual agenda at the personal level is the easiest and most identifiable of the multiple agendas both to understand and to address. Once the executive understands that she must incorporate how her dream for the organization will positively affect the individuals in the organization, she is actually better positioned to make the dream a success.

As the executive begins to prepare for taking her dream public, she must consider the ramifications for the individuals who make up the body of the organization. What is in it for them? How will achieving the dream benefit them? In real terms? In less tangible terms? What does the executive need to do in giving breadth and depth to her description and understanding of her dream to ensure that others can and will see the benefit for themselves?

How long does the executive believe it will take before the organization begins to see progress toward achieving the dream? What can the employees expect in the meantime? What adjustments may they have to make to achieve this greater, grander vision for themselves and for the organization?

By using her understanding of the dual agenda, the executive is positioned to present her dream in such a way that the individuals in the organization, too, will see what she sees. Through her incorporation of how the dream will be of benefit to them, she will gain earlier and stronger support for what it is she wants to do.

It is, once again, important to remember that the employees at all levels—from executive staff to line employees— have experience in other venues. This experience, more often than not, leads them to question and look to disprove steps that executives and management take toward what is said to be "for the betterment of the organization."

To many, this spells cutbacks, layoffs, or reductions in salary, raises, or bonuses. In some way, management improvements are too often seen to be management excuses to hurt the employees — usually, from the uninformed perspective of the employees, in order to benefit senior and executive management.

The executive must be prepared for this response to her dream. She must understand that it has, in fact, nothing to do with her dream for the organization, per se. It is simply a by-product of previous experiences and still existing fears.

As long as the executive factors these experiences and fears into her understanding of the individual's dual agendas she will be positioned to take the advantage. She may, in preparing to go public, need to think back about the steps that she is perceived by the employees to have taken at some past date. If the outcomes were perceived as negative, whether by the employees, the management, or the executive herself, she must be prepared to address how the intent and the outcome did not accomplish her goals.

This is when Executive Thinking is at its best, both in its design and in its outcome. The executive, in knowing that each and every individual will have a real stake in the process as well as the outcome, will be able to speak to the ways by which this thinking-to-action process will differ from previous change and participatory programs; how the management and employees will, in fact, be determining the details of how the dream is to be achieved; that the dream that starts out as belonging to the executive will, ultimately, belong in concept, intent, and action to everyone within the organization.

This is a benefit-based understanding of how the dream impacts the organization. For the executive, in assessing and addressing where things have gone wrong in the past, she is truly learning and benefiting from past mistakes. For the employees, not only do they provide the organization with the benefit of their knowledge and understanding, but they also benefit, themselves, from the implementation of the same.

ڡٯڡ

Organizational Agendas and Executive Thinking

Organizational agendas are more complex and more adversarial than individual agendas. While organizational agendas are driven by the agendas of the individuals involved, they are usually less easy to identify and can do far greater damage to the organization as well as to the dream of the executive.

Organizational agendas pit function against function, department against department, and division against division. They are, most often, an outgrowth of unintentionally competing measures by which the executives and management presiding over the given areas operate. As such, divisive organizational agendas are not intentional, just destructive.

Executives and managers, like line employees, will always work to achieve what they understand to be the goal of the executive and for the organization. Usually, that goal is somehow measured and rewarded within the organization.

If time is the measure, the schedule will be kept—often no matter what the impact on quality or the costs of overtime, materials, and other expenses. If cost is the measure, expenses will be lowered—often no matter what the impact on productivity, quality, or schedule.

In preparing for communicating his dream and for the advent of Executive Thinking throughout the organization, the executive must think about how his organization is managed. What are the measures of the organization? Who controls what those measures are and how they are implemented? What types of analyses have been done on those measures in the past? How often are they reviewed and revised?

To understand the impact of the measures and why the organization operates as it does, the executive must look at and analyze the reward and recognition systems. What are those systems? How do they operate? Are they arbitrary or are they based on the performance measures cited above? What has the impact been of the reward and recognition systems in the past? Have they operated as it was hoped and planned? Based on what indicators?

The more the executive looks at these potentially destructive forces in the organization, assessing how they have manifest themselves and impacted the organization in the past, the more he is prepared to address what must be addressed to successfully communicate and manifest his dream. He can be assured that the rest of the organization will immediately look to the discrepancies between his dream and how the organization works. By being prepared to address the operating systems of the organization, the executive also begins preparing himself for the first levels of communicating the dream and expanding the thinking process.

The executive must go back to the first two ground rules established in the dreaming process. He must understand that there are no wrong answers. He must also suspend disbelief.

In this case, utilizing the first two ground rules during his assessment of the organization and its operation, he is able to objectively look at the organization and understand both how and why it has operated as it has in the past. If the organization had not been able to succeed, it would not still exist. No matter that it does not yet operate to the executive's dream. That will happen.

First, the executive must understand that congratulations are due to him and to the body of the organization for the miracles they have wrought. After all, look at all the organization has achieved despite the problems and difficulties that are so apparent in hindsight.

It is also important that the executive look at his organization dispassionately and without blame. Decisions that were made in the past were made for good reason. Those decisions were also made with the best information available at the time. The intentions were good.

It does not matter that those decisions might not be as applicable in the present or in setting up the organization for the successes of its future. But the executive must be able to look, himself, and be prepared to hear from others about the sometimes unimaginable things that are going on within his organization.

One executive described this process as "having the organization's dirty laundry hung out in public. It isn't that we didn't know it was there. We just didn't look at it in quite the same way." That way was objectively and with an eye toward how those operations could impede the progress toward the achievement of the executive's dream.

The more the executive understands the agendas, both at the individual and the organizational levels, the more able he will be to avoid the same mistakes and to address problems before they occur. Moreover, and most important for Executive Thinking, he will be prepared to listen to and take the advice of those within the organiza- tion who live with the problems on a day-to-day basis.

ℰ☉ℒ

A Battle or a Dance?

The executive has a choice regarding the way she pre- sents her dream—from the start and on an ongoing basis—to the organization. Based on her choice and de- meanor, it can be a battle or a dance. In both cases, there is a leader and a follower. However, the tone, intent, and sometimes the outcomes are radically different.

For many years it has been very popular to incorpo- rate the writings of Sun Tzu, Miyamoto Musashi, and Machiavelli into the reading and training requirements for management. Their books, *The Art of War, The Book of Five Rings,* and *The Prince,* respectively, present a strategic view of manipulating people and situations toward the best outcome for the reader. In each, particularly in the ways that these writings have been interpreted for business, every situation is ultimately viewed as a battle or war. There is a clear delineation between those who are on your side and those who are your adversaries.

There is great power and strength to these writings. In preparing for and addressing competitive situations there may be no better writings to provide a philosophical as well as tactical understanding of the steps that can be taken. The books provide the reader with a veritable arsenal of strategic and tactical options as well as a competitive thinking process that has had a powerful impact on the way businesses do business.

The problem is that many executives and managers, in applying their learning, did not make the differentiation between business adversaries and the members of their own organization. Each person and situation began to be treated as a battle that had to be won—through conflict or guile, whatever it might take.

Unfortunately, in applying this competitive, adversarial thinking and managing process, a tone has been set in many organizations that there are different sides within the same organization. Many executives and managers, in applying their strategic, competitive learning, have not understood that they have done damage to their ability to achieve the very thing they set out to do.

At all levels within the organization people have learned to be wary. People have learned to believe that there are competing management agendas within the organization. They have also learned that, as long as they belong to a particular department or function, it is in their best interest to view the rest of the organization competitively and as adversaries—the way they believe their managers do.

For the executive embarking on Executive Thinking, this must be one of the first tonal issues that she is prepared to address. It is not in the best interest of the organization for people to view the organization as having different sides.

The hallmark and a benchmark of a truly successful organization is each employee's knowledge of and commitment to the goals and dream of the organization and its executive. There can and must be only one side to the organization.

Probably one of the best known and most frequently cited examples of this phenomenon is the United States' space program of the 1960s. President John F. Kennedy had set as his and the country's goal that the United States would put a man on the moon by the end of the decade. This started an acceleration in space and related technology research and development the likes of which had never been seen before.

A story is told about a team of researchers who were studying the NASA organization, looking at its amazing productivity, and trying to determine how and why this was being achieved. The story goes that, in the course of their interviews with employees throughout the organization, in all functions and at all levels, they interviewed a custodian who was sweeping the halls at a late hour. After the team members asked this gentleman what his job was, he responded, "I'm putting a man on the moon."

His sense of his job and its importance was unassailable. He knew what the organization was responsible for and he knew that, as a part of that organization, he, too, had the same responsibility. Because of his commitment to the goal and the actions he was taking, he would also be able to celebrate in the organization's outcomes and his part in their achievement.

For an organization to succeed there can be only one side—the side of the executive, her dream and goals—as the definition and direction of the organization itself. There must be absolute clarity to the understanding of what the dream and goals are and how each individual adds his talents, in both thought and action, to the achievement of that dream.

There can be no room for internal adversariness. The executive must be vigilant in ensuring that no such competitiveness exists. She must work with her associates to identify where and how adversariness exists and determine what can and must be done to address it. She must look to the structure and operations of the organization—both formal and informal—to identify opportunities to reduce adversariness. She must be prepared to listen to and address the input of employees throughout the organization when such counterproductive activities are identified.

It is useful for the executive to think of the "battle" within the organization not as a competitive or adversarial activity, but as a dance. In so doing, the same previously competitive and adversarial actions become part of a larger choreography wherein each person performs his steps while always knowing that his part is a part of the larger dance. That choreography is designed and determined by the executive.

In a ballroom dance or in a ballet, the dancers must know where all the others are on the floor. They are not in competition with one another for space. They know the others are there and why they are there.

In the case of a ballroom dance, they use the space for their greatest enjoyment, neatly avoiding the feet of their partner and the backs of the other dancers. They maneuver around the room, knowing the parameters of the space available, looking for opportunities and taking those opportunities—always to the greater enjoyment and success of themselves as well as their partner.

In a ballet, the dancers all know their place and the places of others. They study the overall choreography to ensure not only that they are in the right position but that they are not getting in anyone else's way. They understand that each move is important and must be done to the highest level of capability and performance. They also know that if their capability and performance are such that they deserve the promotion, they will be moved from a position in the corps de ballet to that of a soloist and eventually a principal dancer.

In the organization's dance, by performing to the top of his capabilities each person works not only to the benefit of the larger organization but to his own benefit as well. This is not by accident but by design—the design of the executive in her role of organizational choreographer.

In all cases, the greatest outcome is enjoyment. The dance takes skill and practice. It also takes cooperation and coordination with others.

While the dance is in progress and when it is over, there is a sense of freedom and accomplishment. Whether that accomplishment is individual or organizational, each person has participated in something bigger than he.

As the leader and choreographer of her organization's dance, the executive ensures that each person has enough space to maneuver, knows his position as well as that of others, and prepares for eventualities that might change the needs or style of the dance. In so doing, each individual, including the executive herself, is ensured a successful outcome.

60

ꙮ

Preparing to Go Public with the Dream

Probably the most challenging moment for the executive is the moment she first speaks her dream to her immediate associates. Up until that point, the dream has been a very personal entity. It has belonged exclusively to the person who dreamt it—the executive herself. While it was all hers, she could change it or maneuver it in any way she wanted at any given time.

In the process of going public, the executive not only exposes her dream to the elements—the opinions and actions of others—but gives up the ability to fully control the dream and its outcome. The dream now begins to belong to the organization and all of its stakeholders.

Of course, this is for the good. The executive knows this. However, it does not mitigate the concerns and, sometimes, the fears of the executive in having her dream exposed to view.

First, the executive must understand that no one is going to ridicule her dream—neither to her face nor behind her back. The listeners will express concerns and offer questions. They may not believe in the dream when it is spoken, but that, too, is to be expected. If all of the people listening to the dream immediately and unanimously voted their unquestioning confidence, the executive would have to be concerned about the truthfulness of her associates.

It is healthy for those who are first listening to the executive's dream not to believe it. For them it is new. The concepts and plans, even if they have been discussed or tried before, are being presented and will be enacted in a different way than previously. They are also being presented in a far more personal way for the executive and, ultimately, for all those who are housed by the organization.

Think of the Martin Luther King, Jr. "I Have a Dream" speech. Not everyone who listened to that speech at the time necessarily believed or agreed with what King was saying. The speech has remained a rhetorical cornerstone, however, not only because of its content but also because of the belief and sincerity with which King described his dream and his belief that it would be achieved.

This is the primary challenge for the executive. In preparing to take her dream public, the executive must be able to present her dream in a simple and elegant way so that her listeners know what she is saying and why. She must be clear in explaining that how the dream will be achieved will be inclusive—everybody will be involved.

She must explain that the dream is a thinking dream. It consists not only of the actions that will be taken but, more important, of accessing and utilizing the thinking and creativity of everyone in the organization.

In describing her dream, she must be so prepared that, during the description, it is almost as if she can touch and feel the dream in its existing form—as if it already does exist. The executive must remember that the dream is her Vision For the organization. It is an active dream both in the present and of the future.

For the executive, the dream is holistic and in Technicolor. It encompasses every aspect of the organization and how it operates. In explaining it, however, she must initially present it in its simplest and most straightforward form.

Thinking in terms of simplicity and elegance of line is the easiest way not only to describe the dream, but also to work toward its acceptance. Simplicity and elegance are easy to understand. They are not jarring to the listener. They may present themselves as almost too simplistic, almost elementary. That may be to the good. The clearer the picture the executive presents, the more likely her listeners will understand what it is she is describing.

This is not to say that the dream is not presented in a comprehensive form. The listeners should be allowed to hear the whole of the dream from the first. Particularly at this first voicing, they must be given the opportunity to see the impact of the dream in its completeness.

Anything less than a comprehensive view is potentially damaging for the executive and to her dream. The listeners should not be surprised at some later date by a piece of information that they then perceive was withheld by the executive. Should that be the case, they will become and remain concerned that the executive is setting them up, that there is some other agenda at play.

In contrast to that perspective, the executive knows that from the first voicing, her intent is to eliminate alternative agendas. She is creating one side.

The description of the dream should not be confused with a mission statement or with an advertising slogan. The executive is not presenting "spin" or manipulation. She is presenting a substantive, achievable description of the organization and how it will operate.

Due consideration and credit must be given to the accomplishments of the organization and its people to date. Too often the dream is lost because the people who are listening do not feel that they have been acknowledged for the things they have been doing and continue to do for the organization. In presenting her dream, the executive must acknowledge and voice her appreciation for what has already been done. She must clearly state that without these accomplishments the organization would not now be in a position to move forward toward the achievement of the dream.

The executive should not worry about how long it will take to describe her dream. It has taken a long time for it to develop. It plays an important role in the future and success of the organization. It deserves airtime.

The executive should be prepared to repeat herself. People do not take in information the first time they hear it. They need repetition and examples. The executive should be able to bring people back to the dream from any perspective or position throughout her explanation and the questions that follow.

In being repetitious, the executive must understand that she probably will bore herself and believe that the redundancy is not necessary. Until such time that the executive is hearing—and seeing—her dream from her associates, she cannot be assured that they have either heard or understood what she has been saying.

The executive must be patient. She, herself, is ready to go. The dream has been germinating for a long time. She has worked long and hard on its development as well as on her ability to speak to and describe it. She knows it is for the good of the organization. She wants it and she wants it *now*.

She must understand that others will, by nature, be hesitant. They will want to know and assess what is in it for them. They will have to think about what part they will play in the dream and how the dream may affect them and their career.

They will wonder the extent to which the executive will hold firm to her spoken dream. After all, they will think, executives have presented dicta in the past and those haven't stuck. They will assess and determine the extent to which they believe that this executive will hold firm in this case.

They will have to plan for their actions and their words. They will want to look at the actions and words of others to determine their positioning. They will want to think about whether this organization, as it is being described in the dream, is one in which they can survive and thrive. They will utilize their own executive skills to determine their actions.

From the executive's perspective, particularly in the first public voicing of her dream, she must not mistake this natural hesitation for a lack of support. Indeed, if her listeners are quiet and thoughtful, she has achieved her goal. She has begun expanding the thinking process to include those with whom she works most closely.

And in that first voicing of the dream, the executive will move toward its achievement through concerted action, first by her immediate associates and then, ultimately, throughout the rest of the organization. The dream is now public. Its success, as well as the success of the organization and all of its stakeholders, has begun.

EXECUTIVE THOUGHTS

For an organization to succeed there can be only one side—the side of the executive, his dream and goals—as the definition and direction of the organization itself. There must be absolute clarity to the understanding of what the dream and goals are and how each individual adds her talents, both in thought and in action, to the achievement of that dream.

It is useful for the executive to think of the dynamics within the organization not as competitive or adversarial activities, but as a dance. In so doing, the previously competitive and adversarial actions become part of a larger choreography wherein each person performs his steps while always knowing that his part is a part of the larger dance. That choreography is designed and determined by the executive.

The executive must be able to present his dream in a simple and elegant way so that his listeners know what he is saying and why. He must explain that the dream is a thinking dream. It consists not only of the actions that will be taken but, more important, of accessing and utilizing the thinking and creativity of everyone in the organization.

66

Commitment

PART TWO

CHAPTER 4

ALIGNMENT

AND SO IT BEGINS. THE EXECUTIVE is now prepared to hold the first meeting with his immediate associates to discuss his dream and where the organization is going. He can describe the dream in detail and can speak to how it will benefit the listeners as well as the rest of the organization. He understands and addresses their skepticism, indeed welcoming it and explaining that it is a healthy and necessary part of the process.

He may choose to discuss the ground rules, at least the first two, as he enters into the discussion. He explains that this time and this process are different—because they must be. He explains that this is his dream for the organization and that, more than anything, he wants those involved in this first meeting as well as, eventually, the rest of the organization, to be a part of that dream.

He speaks to the journey on which the organization is about to embark. He describes it as a dance rather than as a battle. He speaks to the tone of the organization.

He congratulates the organization and all those involved on what it is that they have done. He acknowledges and acclaims their help in the past and for the future. He engages his listeners as a crucial part of the Vision For the organization—now and in the future, a part of the dream.

He describes the pictures in his head—his dream, his goals—so that the listeners begin to see the picture. He engages their imaginations and explains that they will be artists, too, giving further color, breadth, and depth to the pictures being described—now to be their dream and their goals as well as his.

By setting such a tone from the first, the executive has begun to establish that one side, the side of the organization, that is so necessary to the successful achievement of the dream. He aligns himself with his associates and they with him. Moreover, he aligns and includes them all as a part of the dream and its success. He acknowledges and requests their thinking and thoughtfulness and, with the description of the dream, begins pointing their thinking in the direction and toward the actions he needs. Executive Thinking has begun.

≈⊙≈

Creating a Human Collective

There is an interesting character that was introduced in the Star Trek series sequel, "Star Trek: The Next Generation." That character, portrayed as one of the most compelling and dangerous villains, is the Borg.

The Borg is described as a hive containing mutant beings that are part biological and part technological. In integrating a new being into the hive, the being goes through a process whereby his individuality is systematically removed. Ultimately, while becoming this techno-being, his mind and thinking are reduced to being only a part of the one—the Borg.

For those beings who are Borg, there is a certain comfort in being a part of the hive. They are connected to a single knowledge source. As a result they are clearly directed and understand what they are responsible for achieving. They do not have to think for themselves—and, in fact, are consistently and summarily punished if they try.

For those beings who escape from the hive and regain their individuality, there is a period of disorientation and anger, even loneliness. Often, the beings resent the separation from the comfort of the one. Even if they choose to separate from the hive, they are uncomfortable with the responsibilities that come with individual thinking and action.

This is the challenge for the executive in introducing Executive Thinking to her organization. In effect, even with the multiple agendas at play, many of the individuals housed within the organization have developed a Borglike thinking process. They look to whoever holds a more senior or the most senior position and simply do whatever it is they believe they have been directed to do.

Sometimes this manifests itself in the form of the "yes-men" of the organization. These beings, men and women both, have learned to say whatever it is they believe their executive wants them to say while they are in the executive's presence. What they say and how they act once they remove themselves from her presence may or may not be a very different proposition. It doesn't matter. In either case, the yes-men can unintentionally sabotage the dream before it gets its chance for achievement.

They do so by intentionally not bringing their knowledge, experience, and creativity to bear. It is not that they do not have the ability or the depth and breadth of thinking to be able to contribute. It is that they choose, for whatever reason, not to do so.

By taking the most comfortable route, that of the ongoing "yes," they actually steal from the organization and from the executive. They steal the ability of the organization to succeed by having and being able to incorporate greater thoughts and actions into the accomplishment of the dream.

For those executives who are aware that they have yes-men among their associates, particular attention must be paid to accessing their thoughts. Immediate and unilateral agreement to the dream must be considered suspect. Questions must be asked and dialogue must take place. The executive must be assured, in herself, that those with whom she is working to achieve the dream really are on the same side.

In holding this first meeting with her associates, the executive must structure her presentation of the dream as well as her questions to her listeners so that she clearly identifies the yes-men. She must clearly state that she not only expects questions and challenges to her dream but she insists on it. She does not expect everyone to see what she sees immediately—and because her listeners are far more conversant with the body of the organization than she, they are responsible for identifying where the dream may run into problems or may not fit the organization as it stands today.

This, she explains, is all for the good. The more the executive and her associates can identify what needs to be done, the easier the expansion into the organization will be. As important, the more this group gets used to being challenged for the good of the organization, the better prepared they will be to set that tone across the organization.

This engagement and openness to dialogue establishes the tone of the organization as a thinking entity. In contrast to the Borg, it is the executive's and her associates' goal to establish a Human Collective. This, too, is a hallmark of Executive Thinking.

A Human Collective has a sense of community. Each individual knows that he is part of something greater, something more important than he could achieve using only his own resources.

A Human Collective has a sense of purpose. As a community of individuals, each knows what he has to achieve and that he is crucial to the larger organization's ability to succeed in so doing.

Each individual in the Collective utilizes his own knowledge, skills, and ability not only in his own job, but also in working toward a greater good. He brings his thinking to bear not only on how his actions affect the dream of the organization, but also on how his actions interact with the actions of others.

The executive, in establishing this Human Collective ideology, this sense of community from the start, brings her immediate associates in as respected colleagues. Although she and they know that hierarchically they are separated, as a part of the same organizational community they are equals. The executive communicates and demonstrates her respect for and trust in her associates. She also demonstrates that she expects the same from them.

〇〇〇

Beginning the Dialogue

From the outset, the executive must position the meeting as a dialogue. Those who are listening must know that they are responsible not only for hearing what is to be said, but also for responding to and eventually acting upon what is being presented.

The executive's associates will be the ambassadors of the dream. They will be the more frequent and available voice into the organization regarding the dream. They will describe it. They will answer questions about it. They will continually assess not only how their part of the organization is doing toward its achievement, but also what more can and must be done to accomplish the goal.

The dream, after being voiced and discussed, becomes the dream of the listeners. The executive must position the dialogue so that all listeners are given the opportunity and the responsibility to respond. They must speak to how they believe they and their part of the organization will be affected by the dream. They must speak of their qualms and perceived potential pitfalls.

The executive must be a great listener. He must monitor his responses so that his listeners understand that he wants the input, values the information, and will work with each associate to ensure his or her success. The executive, in establishing the dialogue, becomes the first and greatest supporter for all those who support his dream.

The executive is listening for more than his associates' actual words. He is listening for their alignment. As his associates speak, he tries to determine whether they fully understand what it is he described. Whenever necessary, he brings them back to the dream, explaining, sometimes again and again, what he envisions. He asks them to expand upon the ways by which what they are describing gives greater depth and breadth to the dream.

As he listens and they engage in the dialogue, the dialogue expands across the group of listeners. Initially, the executive may find, or purposely structure, discussion to be individual. One at a time the associates speak to the executive with their questions and qualms, their input and understanding.

As the discussion continues and each associate speaks, the executive will find that the group is targeting the discussion more among themselves than to the executive. Bravo. This is the turning point.

In order for Executive Thinking to succeed, the standard steps will be first downward and then across. In effect, these are the dance steps the organization takes while performing its Executive Thinking.

Beginning with the dream and the executive's communication of that dream to his immediate reports, it is understood that, while the dream and goals are universal for the organization, they began with the executive. As such, the executive always retains ownership of the dream—no matter how many others join him in that ownership by their thoughts and actions. He is vigilant in both overseeing and nurturing the dream. He expands it and learns from the actions of others the myriad other ways by which it can be expanded. The steps are continually downward and then across.

Eventually, as the process expands through the organization, there will be a reciprocity in that flow. In a fully implemented Executive Thinking organization, the steps are both upward and downward as well as outward at every level. Everyone is involved.

In participating in the discussion, the executive calls upon the executive skills of his associates. Rather than allowing them to limit their thinking to their segment of the organization alone, they are asked for broader opinions. Each is asked to think as a chief executive officer (that is, the strategist), a chief financial officer (that is, the financier), and a chief operating officer (that is, the tactician). Wherever possible and appropriate, each is asked to think as a nonmanagement member would think. How might he or she react? For what should the organization be prepared?

Organizational Complexity and Executive Thinking

The best way to assess and determine what the organization should be prepared for and how it will react to the dream and its manifestation is for the executive and her associates to look to the organization's present and past. Almost all the necessary information is available through an objective assessment of any changes the organization has made—no matter how comprehensive or limited in scope.

Because organizations are made up of people and most people are uncomfortable with change, most organizations have a history of difficulty in any change process. This is further exacerbated by the complexity of the organization. No matter how large or small, once an organization expands beyond the one person who started it, complexity becomes a challenge.

The executive must remember that she is, through her dream, creating a simple and elegant line for the organization. This simple and elegant line is as free from complexities as it is possible to be. To whatever extent possible, the executive and her associates must assess and analyze how the current complexities of the organization might affect the ability of its people to manifest the dream. By looking at previous changes, or even changes that are currently in progress within the organization, the executive

79

and her associates will be able to identify real and potential obstacles to the dream.

The changes can be as simple as those altering a specific policy or procedure. They can also be as complex as the adoption and implementation of a complete organizational retooling, whether human, mechanical, or informational. In all cases, the changes are made more complex by the complexity of the organization.

The easiest way to begin identifying where those complexities exist and how they affect the organization is by discussing where the listeners' frustrations come from as they try to get business done within the organization. These frustrations are, in fact, indicators of dysfunctional operations within the organization. They are not intentional. They occur because there are obstacles to the completion of what the executive or her associates have asked. These are the manifestations of the organization's complexities.

Sometimes the frustrations come from the structure of the organization. Looking at how information is communicated, decisions are made, and actions are taken most easily identifies those structural obstacles.

Structural obstacles are not always a result of or have to do with the number of organizational or hierarchical levels. It is too easy to blame complexity on the physical structure of the organization alone. Team-based, flat organizations can and do demonstrate as many bureaucratic deficiencies as do the most bureaucratic of organizations. Structural obstacles are action related. The executive and her associates may at some point decide to restructure the physical conformation of the organization. This should occur only with the understanding of which actions they are trying to change, how the existing physical conformation of the organization affects those actions, and what effect the restructuring will have toward the desired outcome.

Frustrations that come from the operations of the organization can be identified most easily by identifying inconsistencies and lack of coordination within and across departments and functions. These are not usually intentional. They do, however, inhibit the organization from being able to achieve its goals.

As the executive and her associates discuss the organization's past and present performance, they must identify and address where there may be adversarial or competitive agendas in play. Looking at the actions of a function or between functions that are causing frustration to the executive or her associates will determine whether there are, in fact, agendas in play that work against the organization. The executive and her associates will then be able to identify areas that are potentially hazardous to the successful achievement of the dream.

Beginning with the first dialogue, the executive must engage her associates in an analysis of where the complexities exist and how they affect the organization's operations. Further, they must discuss the dream in the context of those complexities.

This is an objective discussion. There is no blame assessed, nor is there any need for blame. Like all decisions, organizational complexities result from actions taken on the basis of the best information available at the time. By the time the organization gets used to the change, it has become transparent within the organization. Management and employees view the new complexity as another part of the way the organization does business. It is neither good nor bad. It simply is.

In order to ensure the successful achievement of the dream, the executive and her associates must be relentless in their search for the visible and invisible complexities of the organization. Some they will be able to identify from the beginning. Some will remain transparent until well into Executive Thinking.

Some complexities may never become apparent to executives and management. It doesn't matter. Those complexities and obstacles will be identified and addressed by the employees as they become involved in Executive Thinking. Executives and management will simply see the benefit of the assessment and actions taken.

Ambassadors and Their Mission

The executive should plan on having more than one meeting before his associates are prepared to go forward as ambassadors for the dream. The executive must feel comfortable with his ambassadors' understanding of the dream. The ambassadors must be able to describe their picture of the dream in such a way that the executive is assured that they do, in fact, see what he sees. They must also be able to speak to the impact and importance of the dream in their particular functional area as well as to what their functional area can do to support and accomplish the dream.

Very likely, the executive will find that the ambassadors have begun discussing how to coordinate their actions. These are Executive Thinkers. They understand both the strategic and the tactical necessities of the dream and will act accordingly. They are on one side. As such, they work as a concerted unit to ensure that their side — the side of the organization — wins.

Sometimes, to make the process easier, the ambassadors view their goal and its accomplishment as their mission. Much like the United Nations, they understand that, while each may have individual goals that represent the needs and responsibilities of their particular area, the ultimate goal is a concerted success.

Should the organization have a mission or vision statement, it should be reviewed in the context of the dream and the goals of the executive and his ambassadors. Should the statement remain appropriate and viable, it should be retained. If not, it should be discarded.

This may seem wasteful at first. It also runs the risk of raising the ire and skepticism of the management and employees of the organization. Ultimately, it is worth the risk.

Great damage has been done to organizations as a result of mission and vision statements as well as how they have been utilized. In an Executive Thinking organization, such damage can and must be corrected. Classic mission and vision statements are also unnecessary when Executive Thinking is in place.

As described earlier, vision statements were created with great purpose and intent. It was the hope of their creators that the organization would see all that it could and should be into the future. As also described earlier, these statements did not have the desired effect.

This lack of effect or often negative effect is even more prevalent in the case of mission statements. Once again, this is not to say that mission statements are not for the good. It is in their implementation and management that the differentiation between a classic mission statement and Executive Thinking becomes clear.

A mission statement is designed to be a descriptive call to arms and an assessment tool at the tactical level. While vision and its accomplishment rest with executive management, mission is the province of functional management and employees.

Mission statements often present factual, descriptive details about why the organization exists and for whom. The statements tend to be multipart, starting with a lead-off statement and followed by a bulleted description of how the mission manifests itself. Trust, loyalty, and shareholder value tend to be cornerstones of such a statement's manifestation.

Unfortunately, in most cases, shareholder value tends to show up first, with components related to the employees showing up later. While this may be factually correct, from the employees' perspective it neither is politic nor demonstrates an acceptable level of management support for or belief in the employees. Too often, employees focus on the placement of the mission components rather than on their content.

Mission statements are often written to the lowest common denominator, ostensibly for their ease of use and understanding. Rather than being rousing and directive, they sometimes have the unfortunate effect of being considered insulting.

Just such a case occurred in the writing and distribution of a United States Postal Service mission. That mission statement is "Do the right thing. Deliver the mail."

For those employees who paid attention to it at all, either it had no effect or it had the effect of making them angry. What, they wondered, did management think they were doing up until that time? Was it, they pondered, management's belief that until the advent of the mission they were intentionally doing the wrong thing?

Clearly in this case, the intent of the mission statement was good. From the creators' perspective, it was a simple, straightforward directive of why the Postal Service exists and what its employees should be doing. Unfortunately, both in the way in which it was communicated and in its actual content, the outcome did not match the intent.

After establishing the mission statement, many organizations have little to no structure for its ongoing use as a directive or an assessment. Mission statements are often found beautifully framed on walls in visitor areas, posted in employee lounges and cafeterias, or printed on the backs of employee badges. In one organization, the mission was printed on the inside of cocktail napkins. That these were not to be used by the employees and would only rarely be seen by the organization's customers had evidently not been considered by the management in making the decision to print.

In contrast, the ambassadorial mission in expanding Executive Thinking to the organization is a living, breathing, ever-expanding activity. Rather than being presented in a static form, Executive Thinking, as executed by the ambassadors and their associates, is vigilant in looking at what the organization is working to achieve and assessing how it is doing toward its achievement.

The ambassadors, in working with their functional area, may choose to use a mission statement structure to document their part of the achievement of the dream. This may include identifying the part their function plays in the greater organization, how their actions will enhance the purpose and outcome of the dream, and the part each individual plays, as a thinking and acting entity, in achieving the greater good for the organization.

In many cases, such an ambassadorial mission, rather than being put on a single page, will require pages not only for description, but also for tracking the actions that support those descriptions. In all cases, the ambassadorial mission should be traceable and trackable.

Any documentation to be used by the ambassadors with their associates should be structured for ongoing use as an assessment tool. As the ambassadors prepare to take the dream further into the organization, they should cooperatively develop documentation that their associates will be able to hold up at each meeting and ask, "How are we doing toward the achievement of our mission? How are we doing toward the achievement of the dream? What might be changed? What can we do differently and better than before?"

Just as the dream will expand and grow over time, so, too, will the ambassadorial missions. In many cases, the changes to the dream will be a result of the input and guidance that comes from the ambassadors and their associates.

The more thinking that occurs throughout the organization, the more likely the changes will be a result of and result in the shared dream. As Executive Thinking grows, so, too will the ideas, innovations, and possibilities for the organization, the executive, and the dream grow.

Attitudes, Behaviors and Organizational Action

For the executive, one of his most important and greatest challenges is to understand the acceptance process that every human goes through. There are, in fact, two schools of thought in this regard. One school states that behavior follows attitude. The other school states that attitude follows behavior. In this case, the executive is best served working with the latter school as his operating philosophy.

The executive is going to be impatient to see his dream realized—even more so once he has taken the dream public. There are ambassadors. They seem to understand and be able to speak to the dream. The executive is ready to go. The challenge is in making sure that the organization really does go where it is the executive intends.

This is a make-or-break point for the dream and for Executive Thinking. If not monitored carefully, there will be a great deal of time spent, a lot of discussion, extensive thinking pursued, and no outcome. Even with the nominal support of the associates as they become ambassadors, the greatest initial obstacles to the achievement of the dream exist as the associates walk out the door of the meeting.

On the other side of that door is another world—the world from before the dream—waiting to take the attention of the executive and his associates. Once that world from before has gained their attention, it will work assiduously to keep it.

There will be the work waiting. People speak of their plates being full. People speak of their task loads as multi-course meals and vertical food on an already filled plate. And they are correct. Work and task loads are excessive. Everyone is expected to do more than ever before, better than before, within tighter timelines than before. This is a competitive necessity.

There will also be those not involved in the meeting who may be obstacles to the dream. People will be wondering what the executive and his associates were doing behind that closed door. There will be great speculation and concern. There will be skepticism about things not even discussed or defined outside the room.

Change will be in the air. Organizations have developed a nose for impending changes. They have also developed extensive defense systems to avoid the changes even before they are implemented.

As a part of the first meeting, the executive must prepare his associates—his ambassadors—for the work challenges they will face. Immediately upon leaving the meeting, they will be tasked with assessing their own work to determine which of their tasks is in support of the dream. They will be asked to identify how those tasks assist in the dream's accomplishment and the value the tasks bring to the organization in its present and future state.

For those tasks that are questionable, the executive will advise his associates that they will be responsible for an ongoing monitoring of their own tasks to determine the value toward the dream. All actions and thoughts must be in direct correlation with the direction now set for the organization—its goals and dream.

The executive understands that he cannot wait for the attitude of the associates to change. He must move them toward that change by having them commit to specific actions even before they have left the meeting. Each associate must identify specific tasks and actions that she will take in support of the dream and that will be reviewed at the next meeting.

It may be in the best interests of the executive and the organization that some of the actions are cooperative. The more and the sooner concerted thinking and action are pursued, the faster the organization will adjust to and adopt Executive Thinking. This will, ultimately, lead to a faster accomplishment of the dream.

Actions must be specific and trackable. Initially, the actions may focus more on assessment of the functional areas than on communication of the dream. The executive must be careful that his associates speak as ambassadors—ready to address problems, having answers at hand, in full support of the dream—before he puts the onus of the dream on their shoulders.

This protects the executive, the ambassadors, and the dream itself from possible misinterpretation and mishap. Too often management speaks of the changes the organization is making before it is prepared for any changes to be made. Plans must be in place and actions already taken before any concerted public announcement is made. In most cases, by that time it is no longer necessary for an announcement to be made. The organization is already doing what needs to be done—and seeing the positive outcomes of the actions.

The Organization's Past and Executive Thinking

Management and employees have become jaded as a result of the imposed change programs implemented in the 1980s and 1990s. Many of those programs, though well designed and well intentioned, became the scapegoat for other problems the organization was facing. Some of the programs simply were not designed well for the purposes of the organization.

The less that Executive Thinking is designed to look like those imposed programs the better. This is most easily accomplished by insinuating the process into the organization rather than creating a rally around it. Not only will this be in the best interests of the organization, but it also most closely mimics the thinking process itself.

Thinking, as an activity and in its ultimate satisfaction, is an insidious process. A person starts out thinking about one thing and that thought leads to another. Sometimes the thoughts are linked. Other times they are not. The mind moves out of its normal patterns and into new arenas. That movement is at the core of Executive Thinking.

One executive, a scientist, describes the standard, unchallenged thinking process as "cow paths in the brain." Cows, she explains, will all follow each other, usually in a single or near single line, moving from one location to the other in a proscribed pattern. They do not know where this pattern came from. They simply follow it. They do not challenge or change this pattern, even when obstacles are in their path. Instead, they will simply stay where they are, waiting for the obstacle to be removed.

Her comparison to the human way of thinking is biologically based. Another executive, one who oversees research and development for a healthcare system, explains that as we grow from infancy to childhood and beyond, our brains develop identifiable protein paths. These paths keep us from seeing all that there is to see with all of the glorious challenge and opportunity that those new thoughts would provide.

When we are young children, the paths do not exist. We take in and process information in all parts of our brain. There is no specific path or direction to the stimulation. In effect, there are no limits. Everything we see is new and has new possibilities. Even those things we have seen in the past have a new meaning and potential each time we look at them.

In contrast, as we grow older we begin to develop identifiable patterns or paths for the information to travel. We no longer use our whole brain to take in and use information. We also learn to limit the stimuli that we accept.

These cow paths of the brain limit our present and our future by being exclusive. We develop thinking processes that keep us from seeing all that there is to see. We limit ourselves by not looking for or accepting the potential that is presented to us.

But, just as thinking is a skill, these thinking paths can be altered and added to. As humans, we are not limited to seeing things in one particular way. We choose to see things in a way that is most familiar to us. We may not even like what we are seeing or doing, but, if it is familiar, we will continue—not realizing that we have a choice.

Executive Thinking brings a process to the organization that forces management and employees at all levels to move away from their cow paths and develop alternate routes. Executive Thinking is a system of identifying and implementing choices. At first those choices may be somewhat limited and, from the executive's perspective, not worthy of the dream. Ultimately, as those alternate routes are developed and new paths pursued, the thinking and associated action will be both representative and worthy of the dream as it was dreamed by the executive.

The past loses its ability to victimize the employees. The past becomes a learning tool, no more, no less. While it is important to acknowledge the past—again, each person and the organization itself should be celebrated for what has already been achieved—the past loses its strength as an antiorganizational weapon.

No longer does the organization work with a "Not Invented Here" syndrome because the employees know that the more that can be learned from others, the farther and quicker they and their organization will move ahead. No longer can employees state that "that is not how we do business" because each employee is continually in the process of assisting in devising and designing new ways of doing business.

Management and employees are proud of the organization's past. They see it as a great foundation on which to build. They know, however, that if there is to be a future for the organization, it will be their present and future actions—their participation in the Vision For the organization—that will ensure that such a grand and glorious future exists.

ℰ☉ℒ

Ambassadorial Expansion and Executive Thinking

Although ultimately everyone in the organization is an ambassador for the dream and a part of Executive Thinking, the detail-level tactical ambassadors within the organization are within the management ranks. These ambassadors are the working ambassadors for the dream. Theirs is a purely tactical life. They and their functions do the work of the dream, in their thinking and, more important, in their related actions.

While the executive will see the results of the dream and its manifestation, the working ambassadors and their staff members will be the ones actively creating the dream's manifestation. It is through their understanding and actions that the tasks associated with the dream and its success are considered, improved, discarded, or maintained.

As the executive works with her immediate associates, she should begin preparing them for their responsibilities in developing the management team—the working ambassadors—for their role. The executive should speak to her ambassadors about the process she pursued in getting them to this point. She should introduce them to the third and fourth ground rules so that they, too, are prepared for the cynicism and skepticism that they may encounter. They must be prepared to be supportive of their associates as they assist them in their process and journey to becoming the working ambassadors for the dream.

She should address the concerns she had about a Borg versus a Collective. In mentoring her ambassadors in their role of keepers of the dream, she must prepare them for the thinking and actions that they may take and how to demonstrate their support to their associates.

The dance steps of which she spoke earlier—downward and then across—become the dance steps of the ambassadors as they work with their functions. Analysis and thoughtfulness are the keys. The working ambassadors must also have the picture of the dream in their heads. They must understand what the executive has dreamed for the organization and how their part—every individual's part—is crucial to its success.

The working ambassadors are understood to be and spoken to as executives as well. They must learn to access all of their skills—not just the ones for which they are regularly paid, but also the skills that they bring to bear on their own lives.

The executive and ambassadors understand that each person, as he gains adulthood, becomes his own executive staff. He acts as chief executive officer when he sets goals and strategy for himself. The goals may be financial, personal, or professional. From wanting to be a millionaire to wanting to marry and have children, no matter what the decision, once a person becomes committed to that goal, he sets strategy and sets out to achieve it.

As chief operating officer, he acts on the strategy and goals he has set. Whether it is deciding what college and which degrees will assist him, or where best to meet a potential mate, he sets out an operating plan and he acts. This is the point at which limitations are assessed and overcome. The individual determines how best to work around perceived limitations and constraints—and sometimes how to forge directly through them.

As chief financial officer, the individual has to find the funding to support and maintain his goals and, eventually, his lifestyle. Whether he is investing for the future or negotiating for a home and an acceptable mortgage rate, he uses his thinking skills to financially direct and support his goals.

As chief executive officer, individuals dream and prepare for action. As chief operating and chief financial officers, those same individuals bring all of their pragmatism to bear and find a way to make their dream come true.

The working ambassadors must be directed to apply their already existing Executive Thinking skills to achieving the goals of the organization. They must be spoken to as chief executive, chief financial, and chief operating officers. They must be given strategic information so that they understand the dream in its context.

They must see the dream as a picture to which they, too, are responsible for adding color, breadth, and depth. Within and for their function, their picture, their vision of the dream, must be as Technicolor as that of the executive and her associates.

All of their concerns must be identified and addressed. They must speak of their qualms and disagreements with the dream. Remember that the dream that will be presented to the working ambassadors is the dream as it has been added to and enhanced by the ambassadors from their discussions with the executive.

The executive must make herself available to work with her ambassadors and working ambassadors. She must be able to answer their questions and demonstrate her support.

The executive must be visible to the ambassadors, the working ambassadors, and the organization at large. She must be seen as actively involved not only in the results of the work being pursued, but also in learning more about her organization and its operations. She must also learn more about the dreams of the individuals who make up her organization. That way, as she expands and enhances the dream, it will be done with the real input from and understanding of those who make up the body of her organization—the organization now of her and their dream.

The executive and her ambassadors may find that certain departments or functions are manifesting the dream sooner than others. She will have to remind everyone that this is not a race and that any and all progress is to be congratulated and celebrated. Her ambassadors will understand that they must look, individually and cooperatively, at each and every functional area to continue to determine the needs of the organization in achieving the dream.

This is an ongoing process. It is not static. Working ambassadors, as they begin to work with their staff members in achieving the dream, will be bringing the concerted knowledge and learning from their functional areas to their respective ambassadors. This begins the reciprocity within the system. It is now no longer a downward and outward dance step, but it is upward as well.

Working ambassadors, before bringing their thinking to their ambassadors, may coordinate with other functional areas. They, too, will learn that each part of the organization is a part of a larger whole. Everyone is on one side. Anything that is done must be done to benefit the whole of the organization. Competition and opposition applied in a destructive form to the organization are no longer tolerated. It is a ballroom. It is a ballet. It is not a battlefield.

It is an organization based on respect and trust, designed to work toward the achievement of a dream. It is an organization of individuals who operate as a concerted whole, no matter how different their functions or how geographically distant their operations. It is a thinking organization, one that knows that the impossible is possible. It is an organization of executives.

The executive always retains ownership of the dream—no matter how many others join him in that ownership by their thoughts and actions. He is vigilant in both overseeing and nurturing the dream. He expands it and learns from the actions of others the myriad other ways by which it can be expanded.

The executive is, through her dream, creating a simple and elegant line for the organization. This simple and elegant line is as free from complexities as it is possible to be.

As humans we are not limited to seeing things in one particular way. We choose to see things in a way that is most familiar to us. We develop thinking processes that keep us from seeing all that there is to see. We limit ourselves by not looking for or accepting the potential that is presented to us. But, just as thinking is a skill, our thinking paths can be altered and added to.

98

CHAPTER 5

TRUST

TRUST IS QUITE AN interesting commodity. Conventional wisdom states that once one has lost trust in another, that trust can never be regained. While this is untrue, it provides a convenient scapegoat for nonparticipation in the dream and in Executive Thinking.

As the executive and ambassadors at all levels go out to the organization with the dream, they will find that the subject of trust is bandied about as the reason why various individuals do not want to work toward the dream. They will say that with the organization's past and the experiences of the employees, it should be understood and accepted that they can no longer trust management to do the right thing.

Sometimes this will be based in fact. Through their analyses and assessments of the organization's past, the executive and his associates will find discrepancies between what was said and what was done. Employees have long memories, particularly for what they view as slights. If they believe that they were done wrong in the past, they will immediately call up that memory as a means of keeping themselves from participating in the present and future.

Organizations sometimes become bitter. Whether through economic downturns or bad decisions, things do not always move as and in the direction the employees would prefer. Neither do they move as the executive would prefer. The employees, however, are not aware of, nor often do they care about, the executive's preferences or expectations about the past. They continue to base their assessment of the executive on his position's trappings. He wasn't affected, nor does he care, they might think. After all, he is still living on Mahogany Row with his stock options and big salary.

The executive must remember that no one has asked the employees to act as executives in the past. Little has been explained to either managers or employees about anything from business cycles and the organization's financials to customer needs. This has left employees with a perception of management and particularly of executive decision making as arbitrary and capricious. This also results in a general lack of trust in the organization, its future, and its commitment to its employees, suppliers, and customers.

This is further exacerbated if the organization has operated to competing agendas in the past. Should that be the case, the individuals in the organization have been pitting their personal agendas and organizational agendas against the personal and organizational agendas of others. Once again, the perception by the employees is of an organization and its management that cannot and should not be trusted.

Ultimately, this lack of trust results in a loss of productivity. Instead of operating with an understanding of the organization and its needs, employees operate with an eye toward the next perceived threat to their job, their comfort, or their way of life. They look at others in their department as potential enemies and at other departments as actual enemies. They view management as being untrustworthy or, if they can be trusted, as being ones who will move out of their function in the near future. Therefore, it is best not to put too much faith and hope in one's manager, even when that manager is seen as being "good."

The perception of untrustworthiness is not limited to employees. Often managers view each other with distrust, again usually based on the existence of competing agendas within the organization. How can a manager trust her colleague and co-worker if that person's job is designed to put the manager in a bad light?

Unless addressed, this lack of trust can take a toll on and be a great threat to the manifestation of the dream. It is convenient for those who do not like change to present trust as *the* organizational issue. It is convenient to think and speak of trust as an amorphous entity. That way, no matter what the executive or his ambassadors might do, they cannot reinstate that which was lost. No matter that it was actions that supposedly created the lack of trust in the first place. It is easier and safer to say that nothing that management might do can reestablish the trust that was lost.

Trust as Behavior

Just as trust lost is a result of actions and behaviors, so, too, is trust established or regained through actions and behaviors. It is not true that trust cannot be reestablished. It may take more work than if one starts out with trust from the first, but it still can be done.

In moving forward with Executive Thinking, the executive and her ambassadors must be prepared to establish and reestablish trust in the organization. But first they must know what it looks like so that they can demonstrate it and model it throughout the organization.

One of the finest examples of the manifestation of trust as an identifiable behavior is in the workings of a chamber ensemble. The following description demonstrates both the process and the results.

A chamber ensemble composed of freelance musicians was brought together to perform a Brahms Serenade that had been arranged by the conductor. There were a total of eight musicians besides the conductor. The string section of the ensemble consisted of a violin, a viola, a cello and a string bass. The woodwind section consisted of two clarinets, an oboe, and a bassoon.

The arrangements for the group were that they were to meet at 9:00 a.m. to rehearse and would be playing a concert of the piece that afternoon at 4:00 p.m. Rehearsals would be from 9:00 until 11:30 a.m. and from 1:00 until 3:00 p.m. They would then take a break until the start of the concert.

Most of the musicians had never met. Some of them were seeing the music for the first time that day. The conductor knew the musicians but had not worked with all of them in the past.

The musicians' experience and age varied. Some of the musicians were students of the conductor playing in their first public concert. Some were longtime freelance musicians who made their living playing in concerts, operas, ballets, and Broadway shows in and around New York City. All of them were expert in their instrument.

All of the musicians arrived early. They introduced themselves and began preparing their instruments and music. They checked the seating arrangements and began their warm-ups at their assigned places. They joked with one another, acknowledged each other's playing as well as their mistakes, and commiserated with one another over everything from the early rehearsal hour to the difficulty of the music.

Upon his arrival, the conductor acknowledged each of the musicians and set up his own music. He joked and talked with the musicians, but by this time the musicians had begun to structure their warm-ups toward the music they were about to play.

The conductor began the rehearsal with some personal comments and jokes, thanked the musicians for being there, made sure they all had been introduced, and expressed his delight that they would be playing this premier performance of his arrangement. He then went on to discuss his vision and view of the music.

He explained how he had changed the music from the original arrangement for full orchestra. He spoke of Brahms and what it was that Brahms had wanted to achieve in writing the original piece. He spoke of the particular passages and sections he felt were of greatest importance to the music and the sound that he wanted the musicians to achieve. Before ever starting, he spoke of and described the outcome as well as his belief that the musicians would be able to achieve it.

As the musicians began to play the piece from the start, the conductor interrupted the rehearsal when necessary to ensure the musicians' understanding of the goal. Sometimes he would have a musician or a small group of musicians play a particular line more than once, explaining the phrasing, the nuances, to the musicians before each playing. He would ask if they heard what it was he was looking for.

In some cases the musicians would ask to interrupt the rehearsal for clarification. Whether of a particular note or which instrument should be in the ascendancy, each would ask the conductor to provide guidance and clarification of the piece and his particular part.

Sometimes there were questions about whether the music itself was correct as written. In more than one case, mistakes were, in fact, pointed out to the conductor in the various parts. Changes were made on the spot and the rehearsal continued.

The rehearsal progressed. Some passages were repeated over and over again until the conductor was satisfied that the musicians knew what he was looking for. Some passages were played once and the conductor, although not altogether satisfied with what had been played, would assure the musicians that he believed they knew what he was looking for and would be able to provide it. Some passages were never played at all, with the conductor giving the musicians the same assurances of success.

By the time the morning and afternoon rehearsals were over, the conductor was listening to the musicians not only as they played, but also as they stopped each other or pointed out particular notes or passages in each other's music. He still provided explanation for those passages that required his specific direction or where he did not feel that the musicians were quite understanding his goal for that part. However, by this time, the musicians were actively coordinating amongst themselves, looking to the conductor for overall guidance while looking to each other for direct support and understanding.

When the actual concert took place, the musicians, still new to the music but understanding what the conductor wanted, prepared themselves to play. Prior to the concert during warm-up, there was talk and joking among the musicians while the conductor kept himself separate and apart. Once warmed up and ready, the musicians became silent, waiting for the conductor.

The conductor lifted his baton and the piece began. From that point forward, only when the musicians were looking for specific timing of phrases did they look to the conductor. For all the rest they looked either at their music or toward one another for direction. They nodded and leaned in as they played—giving their colleagues cues and support as needed. When necessary, the musicians would look at the conductor for direction. Otherwise, the conductor looked on, giving direction when necessary but enjoying the music at the same time that he was guiding it.

This is the purest example of trust as it should and can be displayed in any organization of any type or size. The conductor, in the form of the executive, is there to provide the guidance and understanding to those who will do the work. She explains and directs, but she also demonstrates her trust in her associates by not doing their work. The executive must be an executive. She must keep herself separate and apart so that she can always be looking at the whole, while trusting that those who are working with and for her understand not only their parts but also the larger intent of the enterprise.

She must stand back and aside, allowing them to make mistakes while working diligently to assist them in avoiding them. When they do make mistakes, she must be there to support and explain. If the mistake is a result of her actions or direction, she must be prepared to own up to the mistake and work with the associate to make the immediate and appropriate changes.

The executive must understand that she and the organization win when she is not included as a part of the informal network. She accesses in as and when necessary and she is not excluded purposely. However, her greatest accomplishment is in creating an environment wherein colleagues and co-workers look to each other for direction and support. They work together knowing the larger intent without the need for microdirection.

Trust is most clearly demonstrated in an organization when the executive, the ambassador, or the working ambassador steps back and aside, allowing the next level to do their job. They give the individuals the respect they deserve for the work they perform. They respect them for their thoughts as well as for their actions. They treat each and every individual as a valuable entity necessary for the ultimate success of the organization.

ৎ☉৯

The Trust Model: The Behaviors

In order to successfully establish, reestablish, and maintain trust in the organization, a behavioral model must be applied. The behaviors are all visible and identifiable. They are manifest consistently throughout the organization. Within and between departments, functions, and levels, the behaviors are all consistently observable. Across divisions and locations, from manufacturing to service to administrative functions, everybody is assured that they will demonstrate these behaviors and that they will be the benefactors of these behaviors from others.

There are five trust-building behaviors that must be demonstrated. They are *respect, reciprocity, consistency, integrity, and involvement.* Each is equally important. Unless each behavior is manifest, the model will not work. It may have some success, but ultimately it will falter and possibly fail.

107

The executive and his ambassadors must understand that they have a window of opportunity with Executive Thinking that was previously closed. Executive Thinking is about and dependent upon trust within the organization. By instituting Executive Thinking, the executive has the ability not only to assure but to demonstrate to his organization that each individual is valued and valuable. That thoughtfulness and associated actions are valued and valuable. But the only way that the individual's thoughts and actions can be of greatest benefit and success to the organization is if there is mutual trust.

Finally, although the trust-building behaviors are presented in a sequential order, for successful manifestation and results they must be demonstrated concurrently.

Respect

The first of the trust-building behaviors is *respect*. Without respect there can be no real communication or participation. There can be no Executive Thinking. With respect there can and will be a mutual attempt to understand each other—even if the parties involved rest on opposite sides of an issue.

Respect mandates that all employees, no matter at what level, treat others as they themselves wish to be treated. Each person is treated as a thinking, sentient human being, with thoughts and feelings to be valued and appreciated. Ideas and issues are presented in a way that assumes that each person is trying to accomplish the same goal—the good of the organization.

It is understood that not every individual or function benefits in the same ways from the same ideas, but that, too, is accepted and valued. In presenting such potentially opposing ideas, each individual is positioned to take the best from each opportunity and create even greater success across the organization.

Sarcasm and inappropriate humor are not accepted or acceptable. These, too often, are passive-aggressive behaviors used by people who wish to demean others or those others' ideas. Instead, if unacceptable behaviors are demonstrated, the employee is asked to clarify why, in factual terms, she is uncomfortable with what has been said. It is also made clear that such behaviors are neither accepted nor acceptable within the organization.

Respect is manifest in listening behaviors. While in communication with another manager or employee, it is incumbent upon all parties to allow the speaker to complete her thoughts. Interruptions are frowned upon unless they are questions for clarification. Too often a speaker, shut down one too many times, stops trying to communicate at all.

Each individual is given the same level and amount of respect, regardless of her position in the organization. In communication situations between levels, there is often an assumption of respect for the higher hierarchical position, with an attendant assumption of lesser respect for the lower-level position. This can no longer be the case.

In fact, there should be greater respect paid to those who are working day to day on accomplishing the job at hand. As these employees become associates and, ultimately, ambassadors of the dream, the executive and his ambassadors will receive great knowledge and foresight from those on the front lines of the organization.

We have lost many respectful behaviors within organizations. This has occurred in many cases as a result of the growing informality by which organizations work. Too often, informality within an organization can be mistaken for an acceptance of disrespect. Even something as simple as "casual day" often becomes a demonstration of disrespect by employees for their co-workers and their organization.

Suits and ties, dresses and suits physically manifest a formality to the organization that extended to a type and level of respect demonstrated among and between employees. As the wearing of more formal business clothes lessened, so, too, did the manifestations of respect.

It is not that organizations should mandate formal business dress on a daily basis. The executive and his ambassadors must, however, mandate a metaphorical wearing of formal business wear as a means of demonstrating and insisting upon respect within the organization.

People must treat themselves and each other with value and esteem. They must understand that they are ambassadors for their own as well as the organization's mission. As such, they want to gain the greatest respect possible. In order to do so, they must demonstrate the greatest respect for others that they possibly can.

Ultimately, these respectful behaviors lead to a greater understanding and perception of value among and between individuals and functions throughout the organization.

By demonstrating respectful behaviors, each individual has the opportunity to learn from her colleagues, thus building her own abilities.

Reciprocity

The second trust-building behavior is *reciprocity*. Most often and most easily, this is manifest as information sharing among and between departments, functions, locations, levels, and individuals.

Historically, information has been viewed as power. Employees at all levels, from the executive suite to the front line, believed that if they knew something that no one else knew, they held power over the others.

While this was a comforting, although somewhat competitive, thought pattern, it is now patently untrue. As one executive put it, "Information has the shortest shelf life of any product imaginable."

With the advent of technology, the grapevine has become a technological marvel. Information flows fast and furiously, not only throughout the organization but between organizations. Because of the Internet, employees have access to company as well as competitive information that had before been unavailable.

For the executive and her ambassadors, this means that they must be prepared to share as much information as possible as often as possible. They also must assume that a great deal of information that they did not previously believe to be in the hands of the organization is already there.

This assists the executive and her ambassadors in creating an environment wherein reciprocal information sharing is a norm as well as a necessity. As Executive Thinking grows, so, too, will the dialogues throughout the organization expand in scope. Not only will the information be about the organization, its goals, and how everyone can work to get there, but it will also be about that which the employees have found out through their own information-gathering methods.

Information sharing is formalized as part of Executive Thinking. The dream, the organization's direction and goals, its financials, and more must all be shared regularly and consistently throughout the organization. Everyone must know where the organization is going, how it is getting there, and how it is doing along the way. These road markers create a sense of accomplishment. They also build the necessary sense of community.

There must be no perception that information is being withheld or that the process is in any way unilateral. While it will be understood that some information must remain proprietary, it must be felt and believed throughout the organization that that which can be shared is being shared.

The steps of the dance as they progress move in many directions—vertically and horizontally throughout the organization. These dance steps are dependent upon a system of reciprocity within the organization. The executive and her ambassadors must create an environment wherein each individual feels a part of a greater whole. Each must believe that his contribution is valued and valuable to the organization and its success. Each person must ultimately receive some form of reward or recognition for his contribution, whether in monetary or nonmonetary terms. This is the organization physically reciprocating and acknowledging each individual's contribution to the greater good.

Consistency

The third trust-building behavior, *consistency,* is in some ways the most difficult, particularly at the inception of Executive Thinking and the trust-building process. Consistency, whether in trust building or in any other behaviors in the organization, is crucial to the success of the organization and to Executive Thinking. It is also one of the key behaviors that many will be expecting to be displayed and violated.

Consistency is a historical issue. Employees at all levels have lived through many iterations of the organization's development. At each level, promises were made. Many were kept. Many, however, were not. Many that were kept were kept to the employees' satisfaction. Many were not.

Employees have long memories. Some of the actions that caused those memories didn't happen in their current organization or in their current job. That doesn't matter. They transfer those trust issues to their current situation—particularly when there is change afoot in the organization. If they have been in the same organization and those memories are of past executive or management actions, the memories become all the more prevalent and potentially disturbing.

Because executives and most of their ambassadors have been living in their primary universe — that externally oriented universe — they did not, nor do they, see the changes in the same way that their employees see them. Where executives understand that there are business cycles, that programs implemented sometimes don't work, that there are external pressures to which the organization must periodically give way, employees not privy to that information simply see the actions taken as inconsistent. They see the executives and management as being inconsistent. As a result, they believe that neither the executive and management nor their programs can be trusted.

Consistency is equated to trustworthiness. One is trustworthy if one demonstrates the same behaviors consistently. Whether those behaviors are the communication of information across the organization, the active involvement of employees throughout the organization, or the respectful treatment of each individual within the organization, consistency is the key.

No one wants to work in an environment in which they don't know what to expect next. People are uncomfortable with change. When those changes seem arbitrary and capricious or, worse, if they are perceived to apply only to some and not to all, they are viewed as destructive and discriminatory.

A name for that inconsistent environment is the "Shoe Forest." In the Shoe Forest, not only is one always waiting for the other shoe to drop, but one is living in a world of Shoe Trees. These trees are filled with shoes that drop without notice and from any direction. No matter which way you turn, you can always count on a shoe dropping somewhere in your vicinity. And when that shoe drops, it will drop on you.

Inconsistency can lead to fear within the organization. If the individuals within the organization neither know what to expect nor what, exactly, it is that they are supposed to do from one moment to the next, they will choose to do the least possible amount. This fear leads to a paralysis within the organization. And that paralysis is the exact opposite of what must be happening in an Executive Thinking organization.

Sometimes there are concerns that management and employees, through their actions, are trying to hurt the organization. From the first, the executive and his associates must operate with the belief that no one in the organization is intentionally trying to hurt the enterprise or its people. They are all doing what they believe to be the right thing based on the knowledge and understanding they have at that time. As Executive Thinking expands and continues, that knowledge and understanding will grow. Ultimately, the expanded understanding will manifest itself in a reduction of those actions that are unintentionally counterproductive to the enterprise.

In order to create the most trustful environment, individuals at all levels should learn what to expect. If the organization must be fast moving and flexible, then each individual learns that that is the environment within which she will work. If the organization shares information on a regular basis, then the individuals learn to expect information on a regularly scheduled basis. If the organization demands the best from each of its employees, then the individuals within the organization learn that they are responsible and accountable for providing the best to the organization.

Consistency, too, is reciprocal. Just as the employees expect and require consistency from their management, so does management require consistency from its employees. This reciprocity is a sign of respect within the organization. Management and employees alike commit themselves to creating the most consistent, elegant, streamlined organization they can create. They work to the same goals no matter in what function, at which location, or at what level within the organization.

They commit to the organization by behaving consistently so that the organization is able to shift and change as necessary. Consistency, it is understood, and stagnation are not the same. Consistency is a form of trustworthiness. It is a behavioral manifestation of commitment to the organization and its greater good.

Integrity

Whether in information or in action, *integrity* must be demonstrated. Each individual in the organization must assure and be assured that their information, their knowledge, and their actions on behalf of the organization are honest and above reproach.

In information dissemination, report writing, or any other form of information sharing, each individual must look beyond his own agenda to that of the greater agenda—the dream of the organization. Information must be factual and free of bias. Where bias should or must be included, it should be made clear that these are the opinions of the information bearer and not facts in evidence.

Information integrity, and particularly its lack, is another form of the mistaken belief about the power of information. Rather than working with the assumption that information withheld is powerful, each individual must learn that information withheld is destructive to the goals of the organization. The best thinking and associated actions cannot be undertaken if the best information is not available.

Some employees are convinced that information, if reported honestly, will harm them, their colleagues, or their function. This is a tonal issue regarding the integrity of the executive and her organization. An Executive Thinking organization does not assess blame, nor does it punish those who present honest information. Instead, the information is taken as just that, information, and analyzed and assessed accordingly.

Very often what the employees might not know or understand is that just that piece of information about which they are concerned is a crucial piece of a larger puzzle. Where the individual might believe that he is potentially creating harm in communicating that information, he is, in fact, promoting the greatest good—that of honest information sharing and best-informed decision making.

Actions, too, must have perceptible integrity attached. No matter who the viewer, the actions must be seen—and accepted—as being for the greatest good of the organization and with a completely honest and upstanding background and purpose. Consistency plays an important role in demonstrating that integrity. If individuals see that the same actions are applied universally across the organization, the actions are assumed to have integrity.

Integrity in action reduces fear in the organization. Each person knows that he is on the same side. Each demonstrates and sees demonstrated honest, upstanding behaviors, all working to the goals of the organization. Individuals are not punished for their actions on behalf of the organization. Because they are guided throughout the process by their ambassadors, they know the needs of the organization and their role in achieving those needs. Each individual knows that he does not live in a Shoe Forest. He is not always waiting for the other shoe to drop and, as a result, he can and does take the actions that the organization requires to achieve its dream and its goals.

Involvement

In order for the executive, his ambassadors and, ultimately, his working ambassadors to demonstrate their trust in the organization and its employees, they must be actively *involved* in the processes and improvements of the organization. They must be actively and visibly involved in the achievement of the dream.

The demonstrable difference between an organization going through the motions and an organization committed to and succeeding from Executive Thinking is the involvement of its management. This transition from management to associates to ambassadors is the most direct and explicit demonstration of that group's involvement.

The ambassadors must be passionate in their involvement and commitment to the dream. They must speak it and act it consistently throughout the organization. Their decisions must be based on the dream. Their communication with their associates must be toward the accomplishment of the dream. They must believe in it and communicate, through their actions, their commitment and belief on a regular and ongoing basis.

Too many programs are based on a top-down requirement without understanding what happens next. In an Executive Thinking organization, the executive and his ambassadors understand that the top-down part of the process is just the start. The success of the dream is based on the top-down, bottom-up, side-to-side, diagonal, and every other direction commitment and involvement of everyone throughout the organization.

Involvement leads to greater thinking and greater actions. By demonstrating her involvement, each individual becomes a keeper and a grower of the dream. The dream that started out as belonging exclusively to the executive—the picture in his head—is now the province of every associate throughout the organization.

Executive Thinking, in creating a community, also creates a justification for the change of nomenclature from "employee" to "associate." Associates are actively involved in their organization. They are associated with it in every respect—from its dream and goals to the actions that achieve those goals to the thinking and actions that exceed those goals and expand the dream beyond anyone's expectations.

Associates, as involved parties, not only add to but also benefit from the organization and its success. They are rewarded and recognized for their contributions to the organization. They are understood to be of value and valuable to the organization. No matter in what position, every associate is a knowledge worker. It is each associate's knowledge and understanding of the organization, its goals, and how their actions work toward those goals that makes them of greatest value. Not only does the organization not want to lose that knowledge base, but the associates do not want to lose their community. They are, truly, a part of a larger and greater whole that is dependent upon their thinking and actions to succeed.

Involvement at every level creates a sense of the executive in every individual. No longer is she focusing on her particular job or task; she is focusing on the strategic and tactical needs of the organization. She is looking ahead to how else she can be involved, what more she can bring to the organization. She, too, dreams executive dreams. The more passionate that involvement, the higher the return to the individual, the organization, and the society at large as a result of the contributions of all of those who share the organization's dream.

༺◉༻

The Trust Model: The Process

The key to a successful implementation of the trust-building model is the incorporation of the behaviors into each action no matter what the task. The actions must occur concurrently and consistently within and across the organization. Initially, it is the executive and her ambassadors demonstrating the process. As they continue to model the behaviors, as well as not tolerate aberrant behaviors, the trust-building behaviors will be manifest throughout the organization.

In all cases, no matter what the situation or the purpose, each individual within the organization must be treated as a colleague. Think about the chamber ensemble. The conductor had the greatest knowledge about the music. He had arranged it from its original form into the chamber version to be played. He had studied the composer enough to be able to speak to the original intent and purpose of the piece. He knew what he was looking for, but he also knew that he needed to look to others to achieve it.

Each of the musicians was treated as a colleague. Clearly there was a differentiation not only in status but also in who would receive the greatest kudos for the outcome. Ultimately, that didn't matter. The conductor demonstrated his respect for each musician by treating him as a thinking, talented, valuable person integral to the success of the enterprise.

The musicians treated each other with the same sense of collegiality. In any classical musical ensemble there is a mostly unspoken caste system. Strings, and particularly the first violins, are the prima donnas of the ensemble. The conductors most often face them, direct them, pay attention to them. It is the first violinist who is entitled "concertmaster," second only in importance to the conductor himself.

Yet, in the chamber ensemble, which both in size and in scope is directly comparable to the structure of the executive and her associates, no prima donnas emerged.

Each musician knew that he was dependent upon the others to create a success. Even though the conductor tended to pay more attention to the strings, the strings paid equal attention to each other as well as to the woodwinds. The musicians treated each other as colleagues no matter how big their part, how important they were to the piece, or how established they were in the musical community. They were colleagues, first and foremost.

Of course, it is understood that there is a hierarchy in any organization and respect is paid to that hierarchy. However, the key to creating a community of colleagues or associates is to ensure that the hierarchy does not get in the way of the business at hand—the achievement of the dream.

Hierarchy, no matter how flat or multilayered the organization, is simply an organizational fact of life. Bureaucracies and team-based organizations operate to some form of hierarchy. Neither does it nor should it matter in an Executive Thinking organization.

By creating a world of associates, all of whom understand that they are a part of the same goal—a larger goal than just they or their function—an environment of collegiality, mutual trust, and passionate involvement is established. All are ultimately trying to do the same thing—accomplish the dream. They understand that some are more senior than others, some have more experience than others, and some have specific expertise that differs from that of others. Rather than being seen as differentiators, these differences are seen as enhancements to the possibility of succeeding at and exceeding the dream.

Trust comes from a sense of being valued. Being treated as a respected colleague—a thinking entity who adds to the success of the organization—is the basis of that trust. The more and more often executives and their ambassadors demonstrate their belief in the value of each associate, the more successful Executive Thinking and, ultimately, the organization itself will be.

EXECUTIVE   THOUGHTS

Just as trust lost is a result of actions and behaviors, so, too, is trust established or regained through actions and behaviors. It is not true that trust cannot be reestablished. It may take more work than if one starts out with trust from the first, but it still can be done.

The executive must be an executive. He must keep himself separate and apart so that he can always be looking at the whole, while trusting that those who are working with and for him understand not only their parts but also the larger intent of the enterprise.

Executive Thinking, in creating a community, also creates a justification for the change of nomenclature from "employee" to "associate." Associates are actively involved in their organization. They are associated with it in every respect. Associates, as involved parties, not only add to but also benefit from the organization and its success.

CHAPTER 6

DYNAMICS

THE PURPOSE AND OUTCOME
of Executive Thinking is to get the highest return on
everything everyone in the organization does. No matter
what the task or who is performing it, there should be a
direct and positive relationship between that task and the
goals and direction of the organization.

The only way to ensure that that occurs is to ensure
that all employees throughout the organization know
what they are doing and why they are doing it. They must
understand their responsibilities not only in the context
of the task at hand but, more important, in the context of
the larger organization.

Employees, as they transition to true associates, must be asking questions of themselves and of their management. They must be assessing whether they are adding value on a consistent basis or if their actions are not to the real benefit of the organization. They must also be asked questions by their management about their actions and how those actions work to the benefit of the goal—achieving the dream for the organization. As those managers act as ambassadors of the dream, they must continue to access the thoughts of the associates toward the achievement of the dream.

This sounds no different from any number of other initiatives that organizations have experienced in the past. Invariably organizations and their management have committed to programs and processes that were designed to gain just those benefits.

What, then, went wrong? Why is it that organizations committed to the accessing and utilization of all employees' knowledge, skills, and abilities somehow were not able to achieve that goal? Moreover, if the implemented program seemed to succeed, why did it not result in the achievement of the goals that had been set out by the executive at the inception of the process?

The answer lies in the way in which organizations have come to work. No matter how flat or bureaucratic, no matter how technologically advanced, no matter how old or young, organizations—and particularly the employees within them—work from a system of Tribal Knowledge.

Tribal Knowledge and the Organization's Operations

In tribal systems, people know things. They don't necessarily know how they know them or where the information first came from. It doesn't matter. The information conveyed is central to the belief system of the members of the tribe. As a result, when external changes occur, they usually do not last long. Because the belief system remains intact, it is both easier and more comfortable for the tribe to fall back upon what was previously known and accepted. Thus, the changes are short-lived.

This is not much different from the way in which organizations operate. People do things. They don't know why they do them. They don't know where the original direction came from. They don't even know whether what they are doing is being done most correctly or appropriately for the organization. They just know that from the time they came to the organization or to their particular job, this was how they were supposed to do what they do.

They were not supposed to ask questions. They were not supposed to challenge the way things had been done. If they did, they were usually confronted by immediate management or even colleagues from their same work area uncomfortable with the idea of change.

Too often they would be confronted with the response to their idea that there was information they didn't know that made their recommendation unworkable. They wouldn't necessarily then be provided with the information. They would simply be told, and told, and told again, that there was information that they didn't know.

This phenomenon is most apparent when a new employee—no matter at what level—joins the organization. Invariably during the interview process, the candidate is told that one of the main reasons she is being brought in is because of the new ideas and perspective that she will bring to the organization. She is being asked to bring new and different thinking to the organization.

Unfortunately, upon becoming part of the organization, that same candidate with the valuable alternative perspective is consistently pushed to become a part of the tribe. Whether directly or indirectly, the new employee is confronted with an attitude that what she has to say is interesting but not applicable. What she is suggesting may have worked someplace else, but that someplace else is not here. Ultimately, the new employee and the response to her ideas are the embodiment of the "Not Invented Here" syndrome.

This is not a case of bait and switch. The employee as candidate is not being misled by her interviewers. They really do want the new ideas and new thinking brought to the organization. However, once they are confronted with what those ideas might mean and entail operationally, the strength of the previous belief system begins, once again, to prevail.

In effect, the tribal elders, in the form of executives and management—some of whom are no longer with the organization—are still setting the goals and the rules for the organization. Safety lies in sameness. Safety lies in continuity.

There is both a real and a perceived difference between sameness, continuity, and stagnation. Sameness and continuity are often perceived as forms of consistency. They are seen as holding on to the old ways because they are tried and true. They have a track record.

Stagnation is understood conceptually to be a bad thing. As such, in the eyes of the tribe there can be no connection between sameness, continuity, and stagnation. If there were, the tribe members would have to begin questioning those long-held beliefs that have made up their operating systems for so long. As a result, the tribe members of the organization choose not to look at the reality of the situation—that sameness and continuity are leading to stagnation.

Organizations and tribes are not the same thing. Even though they may operate in close comparison, there are real and necessary differences between the two. The first is that the executives of the organization understand that sameness and continuity can be dangerous. They will, if unchallenged, lead to stagnation.

The organization and all of its members also understand that questions must be asked and the old ways must be challenged. Unless those actions are taken and supported, the organization runs the risk of languishing in the old ways and being passed by old and new competitors.

Managers and employees no longer accept dicta as a way of doing business. They understand that they have something to offer. They also know that there are many organizations that are looking for their expertise. They know that Tribal Knowledge as a way of doing business not only doesn't work, but works against their own as well as the organization's agenda.

However, because the previous changes in the organization were based exclusively on actions and results rather than on a full understanding of the thinking and concepts involved—the why of the organization—dicta remained intact. The difference between Executive Thinking and Tribal Knowledge is that each and every member of the organization is not only asked but expected to participate in the thinking. Further, she is rewarded for her alternative views and the actions taken that result in an even greater organization than previously existed.

Thus, Executive Thinking works to move the organization away from the tribal system and actively toward a positively directed, questioning, and challenging environment. The advent of Executive Thinking—in effect, the requirement that every individual challenge the existing belief system—immediately changes the organization's culture away from one that is based in potential stagnation. Instead, the organization is consistently positioned to look for new opportunities and new ways of achieving those opportunities.

Where a system of Tribal Knowledge as applied to the organization keeps people from dreaming, Executive Thinking promotes dreaming. Those dreams are based on an organizational system that supports and assists each individual in achieving her dream. Executive Thinking makes it worthwhile for individuals to challenge their previously held beliefs. Each individual sees that her participation in the system works not only to the benefit of the organization, but to her own benefit as well.

There is no longer any question that cannot be answered. Granted, if the information is proprietary, the answer may be limited—but there is an answer. No longer is an employee told that there is information unavailable to her. Information is available and accessible.

The organization not only supports the ideas and perspectives brought in by new employees, but demands that all employees take an alternative look at what their tasks are and how those tasks are accomplished. Such alternative thinking is prized by the organization. Individuals are given ongoing opportunities to develop their thoughts, bring those thoughts to the table, and work with others in their achievement.

For the executive, there is little risk in expanding the organization's thinking in such a way. The dream provides the parameters for the actions that are taken. Alternative thinking that goes beyond the boundaries of the dream is noted but not immediately acted upon. As the individuals become better versed in the dream and in their part of its accomplishment, they will know that the alternative they are presenting is outside the boundaries. That does not make it wrong or unusable. It is a question of timing.

Executive Thinking abolishes the beliefs that no longer serve the organization. Those beliefs that still hold value to the organization will not, however, be lost. Instead, they will be incorporated into the new ways of thinking—better informed, positively directed, participatively oriented—and given a new and more active lease on life.

Thinking as Motivation

Executive Thinking is based on using thinking as a motivational tool for the organization. Thinking as an action and with its attendant results is a clear demonstration throughout the organization that each person is of value. Each person is shown that what he brings to the discussion—no matter what—is believed to be of use and value to the organization. Each person learns from the others, no matter at what level and no matter in which function. Each person is there in the organization not only to provide his thoughts but to learn from his colleagues and associates.

It is highly complimentary to ask a person what he thinks about a given situation. It demonstrates a level of trust and respect for that person's thoughts. Further, by engaging in dialogue—asking the follow-up questions of understanding, as well as positively presenting an alternative view for discussion—both participants become aware that they and their thoughts are of value. This, then, motivates the participants to continue thinking and acting in concert with their thoughts within the parameters of the dream.

There is a common misconception that people are motivated extrinsically. Whether through monetary or other reward or recognition systems, it is erroneously believed that the people in an organization will be motivated to do more and better because of the rewards that they will receive at the end of that process or action.

This is not, in fact, the case. Motivation comes from within. It is an outcome of an intrinsic desire to pursue whatever the required action might be. Once an individual has determined for his own reasons that this is a direction that he wants to pursue, he will be motivated to continue on that course.

Individuals also rethink their motivations over the course of time. As situations change, each person looks to the actions and commitments he has made to determine whether he is still being best served by continuing in that direction. If so, he is motivated to continue going forward as before. If not, he will change his direction to suit the new information and the new direction he has chosen.

This is not to say that external rewards have no place. It is always a pleasure to be recognized for one's actions. The most common form of recognition historically used by organizations is the reward and recognition system. This system, however, does not motivate. It simply acknowledges actions performed in the known direction of the organization and its goals.

Thinking, in contrast, is a purely intrinsic activity. The only place a person can think is inside his own head. What he thinks about and how he thinks about it can be affected by outside information and stimuli. This makes Executive Thinking both the most potentially motivating and the best opportunity for the individual and the organization.

Each individual brings his own thoughts to the organization. Those thoughts are based on his experiences as well as his beliefs. Some of those beliefs are based in Tribal Knowledge. He has learned the belief system within the current organization or from his previous experiences. He sees things differently and yet the same as many others within the organization.

The executive sees things altogether differently. She is not a part of the tribe even though she is its leader. As the leader she is responsible for ensuring that the organization pursues the correct course. But by virtue of her responsibilities, she must leave the detailed actions to others in the organization. Her view is made up of external indicators from the marketplace as well as from the results of her own organization's actions. She does not see the organization as a tribe member would, nor should she. She does, however, establish the belief system of all those within the organization.

Executives become executives because they can and do think. Executives are already motivated by the ability and the opportunity to think. They create and look for new ideas. They actively pursue new ventures and venues for their thoughts and actions—and their organizations look to them to do just that.

By using Executive Thinking to extend the thinking activities in the organization, the executive is providing every individual the opportunity and the responsibility to gain the same levels of motivation and satisfaction that the executive lives each day. Each person becomes valued for his contributions. Each person is treated as one who can and does bring more to the organization than just a competent pair of hands. Each individual is viewed as an integral part of the larger whole and its success.

For the individuals in the organization, the advent of Executive Thinking allows them to find a voice in the organization. They are no longer told that there are things they don't know. Instead, they are asked what they do know and think, how they would pursue a particular venture. They are asked to find that voice and speak with the assurance that what they say will be treated with respect and consideration.

Thinking is both intrinsic and motivational. Each person's brain moves in its various directions based on the stimulation and information it receives. Thinking can occur only intrinsically. Further, when the thinking results in satisfactory outcomes or sense is found in extending the thinking to look at other possibilities and opportunities, the individual is motivated to continue and expand his thinking and associated actions.

For the executive this is the means and outcome of Executive Thinking. Each person, upon being given the appropriate stimulation and information—the dream and all of its associated information—is then both asked and expected to express his known thoughts and expand further upon those thoughts based on his own experience and the ongoing dialogue. Each individual, through his thinking and the voicing of his thinking, becomes an active participant in the process and the results of the thinking organization.

People across and throughout the organization know what they must think about and, over time and with the information provided, are given the skills to do their highest-level thinking. Each person thinks to his own level and then goes beyond that level to the extent and with the ability he chooses. Each individual is motivated to know and understand more so that better and higher-level thinking can be consistently and continuously pursued.

Thinking is a learned behavior. Each person decides how much he wants to and has to think based on the expectations placed upon him and the belief shown in him. By instituting Executive Thinking, the executive of the organization is making it very clear to every person involved that she believes in and values every individual in the organization. She is entrusting her dream to these people and believing that they will see what she sees and more. She is putting her faith in their abilities and voices to accomplish and exceed the dream.

The executive thinks, knows the value of that thinking, and believes that all associates across the organization can do the same. She asks for their input and pays attention to their thoughts. Based on that input she expects and receives action, and recognizes each individual for his contribution to the organization.

The executive motivates the associates by giving voice to her belief that their intrinsic abilities, heretofore not accessed by the organization, will make all the difference in the organization's present and future. She shares her Vision For the organization so that they see and share that vision. She voices her belief and her understanding that what must be done cannot be done by her alone—nor should it. She makes it clear that each individual plays an important and irreplaceable role in the organization.

By using thinking as a basis of assessment, each individual in the organization is irreplaceable and the executive knows it. Each person brings his own thoughts and abilities to the organization. While those thoughts and abilities may be like those of others, they are of necessity different because they belong to that person alone. It is only that person who can voice his thoughts, beliefs, and recommendations for action.

As an Executive Thinker and budding executive, each individual, by respecting the voices of others, knows that it is the combined voices and actions that make the difference. Each person knows that neither is he alone in his pursuit nor should he be. Also, as he gives voice to his thoughts and beliefs, he is joined in those beliefs by others, even as his beliefs are being augmented and enhanced.

Thinking at all levels becomes the most participatory and motivational of all activities within the organization. Combined with the associated and resulting actions, that participation and motivation can and does consistently increase.

ℰ◎ℒ

Participation and the Victimless Society

One of the purposes of instituting a participatory process is to ensure that everyone has a voice that is heard. As a result, the larger voice of the organization becomes more powerful and representative. The organization and its operations speak to the truth of how the organization operates, what needs to be done, and how to address those needs.

The superordinate voice is the voice of the executive. It is his voice that speaks to the overall direction of the organization, why that direction is important and necessary for the organization's ongoing survival and success, and how he envisions the participation of those within the body of the organization making it possible for the organization to achieve and exceed its goals.

Thus, participation and Executive Thinking are designed to ensure that all voices are heard. This, then, ensures that no individual within the organization is positioned to say that she has not had the opportunity to have a voice and that she is a victim of circumstance.

Unfortunately, because the role of victim has become for many the role of preference, there will be those who use the participatory process specifically as a means of promoting their role as victim. Much like the "yes-men" of the organization, victims choose to abdicate and avoid responsibility by assessing and placing blame elsewhere. These individuals will say that no one wants to hear their voice. That when they do speak they are not treated with respect. That they are not valued. This consciously presented illusion gives them the excuse not to participate in the positive direction of the organization, and justifies their attempts to move in a negative direction.

Victims in an organization are not stagnant. They are in reverse. Any action that they see as moving forward toward a goal that they do not embrace or with which they are not comfortable, they will move to reverse. Being a victim is not a passive role. It is a very active, time- and energy-consuming role. It takes a lot of thought to ensure that one is consistently seen as the victim of circumstance—and to create the environment or at least the question in others that leaves them wondering whether they, too, might end up in the same position.

Victims act on their own behalf, but with a larger goal in mind. They do not want to see occur whatever it is that they decry. Rather than speak to the real issue, however, they use the means and methods of the process that is

138

supporting the larger goal to sabotage its success. In the case of Executive Thinking, this is the voice that says no one is listening. No one really wants to hear. This is just another version of the same old stuff.

For the victim, participation comes in the form of gathering followers to support her stance regarding the organization and its new direction. Wherever and whenever the opportunity presents itself she will point out to others that that was exactly what she was saying. That was what she was afraid of. Don't they see, it is happening to them now as well as to her.

It makes no difference whether there is merit to what she is saying. It is the intent of the underlying voice that is of greatest importance to understand.

Victims are victims for a reason. They do not want whatever it might be changed. They feel at risk if those changes are allowed to occur. The world as they have known it will not be the same. It will become a place of danger and risk.

Even if they know that the organization as it is currently operating is in danger, victims would sooner support the old ways than risk the new. They choose—and it is a conscious choice—to hold firm to the tribal beliefs. They believe that sameness and continuity result in safety rather than choosing to see it as the threat or actuality of stagnation.

Victims are not unthinking people. They are great thinkers. They think about their own safety before anything else. They think about risk. They think about change and how that might affect their safety and risk tolerance. Victims have no tolerance for risk. They choose to hold firm to that which is known rather than risk moving in a direction toward what they perceive as the unknown.

The executive must expect and plan for victims in the organization. In preparing his dream for presentation and discussion by himself and his ambassadors, he must make sure that the direction set for the organization is clear. He must also ensure that the reasons for that direction as well as the expected outcomes are just as clearly stated.

Too often in the past, victims have found a comfortable niche within participatory systems because the direction and intent of the process were not adequately explained. When the participatory system is seemingly directionless, those within the organization begin working to the axiom "When you don't know where you are going, any road will take you there." This provides fertile soil for the victim to grow her army of supporters.

In the case of Executive Thinking—even though it is not presented as a program per se—the mere existence of participation and dialogue will give the victim and her prospective cohorts both the time and the opportunity to blame others and avoid taking any action whatsoever. Again, this is not without purpose. The purpose of placing blame and taking no action is to ensure that the process at the very least stagnates and at best reverses.

Thinking by others is one of the greatest threats to organizational victims. As long as they can position themselves as the ones who know what is really going on, they are assured that there will be others who will follow their lead. In a thinking organization, that power is removed from the victim. Others know the reality in its actuality. This knowledge disarms the victim and leaves her unable to affect the thinking and actions of others.

An organization that adopts Executive Thinking neither can nor does tolerate victims or sabotage. Too much is at stake. Action must be taken to protect the organization and the dream from being overwhelmed by the sabotage effected by those who prefer to be victims.

The executive, in preparing for and supporting the dream as it goes public, must do all he can to ensure that his dream is clear and understandable. He must engage the imaginations of those within the body of the organization. He must present his dream in such a way that every individual in every function at every location not only sees the dream, but also sees how she, too, will benefit from the accomplishment of that dream.

In the participatory process, the trust components must be consistently demonstrated. Each individual must feel respected. Each must have a voice that is heard. Dialogue—always in the positive direction—must be the norm. Questions must be asked and answered and reviewed once again for the potential impact on the achievement of the dream.

The dream must be reiterated over and over again by the executive, his ambassadors, and the associates themselves. They must always have the goal in view as well as the direction they are going to achieve that goal. They must see the dream as a clear picture. As well, they must see themselves as a necessary part of that dream.

By reiterating, clarifying, and building support for the dream, the executive avoids creating victims and provides less opportunity for those who already exist to build support. In effect, the executive makes those who embrace the dream the active participants in the dance. The victims become the wallflowers waiting to be asked, but never the participants. Ultimately, those victims will have to either become dancers or find another dance elsewhere.

The Role of the Executive During Implementation

Throughout the preparation process, the executive has continued to live in her parallel universes. She is still wholly engaged in the external universe to ensure the overall direction and success of her goals. At the same time, she is actively involved in the internal activities of the enterprise to ensure that the organization and all of its members are doing everything they can to achieve those goals.

For both the executive and her ambassadors, implementation of Executive Thinking brings more changes to roles and responsibilities. By looking externally and on the surface at their actions, everything seems the same. They are still responsible for higher-level decision making. They still have the responsibilities associated with the oversight of the organization. They still own strategy and have tactical responsibilities.

Yet, though the roles and responsibilities look the same, they are, in fact, different. From the first time the executive goes public into the organization with the dream, the expectations of and for that executive begin to change. The executive, as she continues to speak to her dream and everybody's part in it, stops being seen as the trappings of her job and begins being seen as a person in her own right.

No longer is the body of the organization looking exclusively to the executive as some sort of ersatz messiah responsible for taking them to the organizational equivalent of the promised land. It is no longer the executive who is seen as having the answers. Instead, it is the associates who see themselves as being the answer to the executive's questions. She knows and speaks to where they must go and are going. They are responsible for the process of getting there. She will support and direct them in getting there, but they are the ones consistently and continually taking the actions that result in the accomplished dream.

Executive Thinking is an extremely active process. The executive, in ensuring that the organization is going where she wants it to go, becomes a very active, visible entity within the organization. At every opportunity she speaks to her dream and to each associate's part in the achievement of that dream. She engages in dialogue with the ambassadors and associates about their thoughts as well as their progress.

She creates an environment within which ambassadors and associates feel comfortable speaking to her as an equal while still understanding and respecting her position within the organization. She speaks to them honestly and expects and receives the same from them. Anything less is unacceptable—and she is clear in so saying.

Positive, constructive conflict is viewed as progress toward achievement of the goal. The executive joins in meetings to ask associates how they are doing toward the dream, what do they see as their part of it, what could she have done to better explain it. The executive asks associates to describe the pictures in their heads. She actively promotes their thinking out loud to her and to others.

Taking the information that the associates provide, she further clarifies her dream to ensure all associates' shared understanding. She recognizes and congratulates everyone throughout the organization for his or her contributions. She pays tribute to the associates by taking their thoughts, actions, and accomplishments and expanding her dream based on their actions and results. She takes the credit due to her, but, more important, she gives credit where credit is due no matter to whom or in what position in the organization.

The executive begins to question some of the ways by which she has participated in the organization's operations in the past. She looks to those tasks that she performs and questions why they are her responsibility. She wonders whether there are others who are now ready to, or who could, with training, take over those responsibilities.

Executives supporting Executive Thinking step back from their organization and question both "Why?' and "Why not?" In asking "Why" they are assessing how things are currently done. They are questioning the means by which they are doing their jobs as well as determining where their understanding of their job and responsibilities came from.

As others bring them decisions to be made, they question what led the decision to be brought to them. Were these types of decisions always brought to them? Do they want to continue to be responsible for making those decisions? How much time is it taking for the decision-making criteria to be prepared and presented to them? Is there anyone else in the organization who can or should be making those decisions? Possibly the person who asked the question?

As the ongoing and most visible role model for the organization, the executive begins preparing herself for the empowerment process that must accompany Executive Thinking. As the members of the organization become more cognizant of their responsibilities in the context of the dream, it is no longer necessary for all decisions to move upward.

Executives become aware that upward delegation of decision making is an often-used victim's tool. By abdicating responsibility for the various decisions and making them the responsibility of the executive, the victim positions himself to point the finger at the fallacy of the organization and its operations.

Sometimes executives inadvertently play into the hands of the victim by using the often-heard threat, "Don't bring me your problems unless you want me to make the decision. I will and you may not like it." This provides the perfect opportunity for the victim to use the executive and her position as an example of why the organization cannot succeed.

Executives will continue to make decisions. They must. They are thinking, action-oriented people who know what needs to be done and have no fear of taking the steps to get there. They are risk takers by trade and by nature.

They are also, in instituting Executive Thinking, trying actively and assiduously to remove themselves from the operation-level decision making that should reside in the operational, functional areas. They must be on the lookout for any opportunities to allow those who are working on the achievement of the dream to take action and responsibility toward its success.

This, in effect, is the "Why not?" assessment process. The executive must look to the current operations at her and other management levels to determine how the organization can position itself for a next generation of its own operation. The concept of reinvention is not one that is new to executives. The executive understands that reinvention of the individual as well as of the organization is necessary to ensure ongoing success.

As the executive begins to see the realization of her dream, her parallel universes will gain even greater breadth and depth. As the dream manifests, the executive will be actively looking for ways to expand the organization's operations in new and different directions. This may require a new organizational structure. A new economic model for the organization may be required. This is the forte of the executive. This is her strength. She neither does nor can rest on her laurels. It is not in her nature. Thus, even as the organization moves into its initial implementation steps, the executive is already light years ahead developing her new dream—the next dream for the organization.

EXECUTIVE THOUGHTS

The difference between Executive Thinking and Tribal Knowledge is that each and every member of the organization is not only asked but expected to participate in the thinking. Further, he is rewarded for his alternative views and the actions taken that result in an even greater organization than previously existed.

There is a common misconception that people are motivated extrinsically. It is erroneously believed that the people in an organization will be motivated to do more and better because of the rewards that they will receive at the end of that process or action. In fact, motivation comes from within. Once an individual has determined for her own reasons that this is a direction she wants to pursue, she will be motivated to continue on that course.

By using Executive Thinking to extend the thinking activities in the organization, the executive is providing every individual the opportunity and the responsibility to gain the same levels of motivation and satisfaction that the executive lives each day. Each person is valued for his contribution. Executive Thinking allows each person to find a voice in the organization.

Collaboration PART THREE

CHAPTER 7

CAUSE-EFFECT

AS WITH EVERYTHING IN LIFE, ORGANIZATIONS work on a system of cause and effect. There is an underlying intent that leads to actions taken. Those actions then lead to an outcome. This is the law of cause and effect.

In instituting Executive Thinking, the laws of cause and effect are particularly in evidence. From its inception, the process must be designed and devised so that the intention is clear and the actions taken are clearly in support of that intention, with the result being as much as, if not more than, what the executive expected.

Dr. W. Edwards Deming, the management theorist, often said of organizations and their actions, "The intent is noble. The method is madness." This, unfortunately, provides an excellent description of what happens when the actions taken by the organization are not, in fact, in alignment with the executive's intent.

In the cases to which Deming was referring, the intention was to improve the organization and its operations. The actions taken, however, pointed in a different direction—sometimes unknown even to the executives and management. The outcome, in keeping with the actions, left the organization floundering in multiple directions, with each individual having a different understanding of what the process was to achieve and why.

By viewing the laws of cause and effect prior to and throughout the implementation process, the organization is positioned—and continues to position itself—for success. Executive Thinking, as an active process based on the dream of the executive, is both a catalyst and an outcome toward success. The process makes the dream a living, breathing entity that manifests itself in all corners of the organization. It creates a positive alignment beginning with the executive's intent and causing the organization to achieve the outcomes desired.

Employees, however, at the advent of the process, will not necessarily see or believe the intent. They will be wary that what they are being asked to do will only lead to a program like those they have encountered before. That is why Executive Thinking must be implemented by infiltration and insinuation. The more invisible the system to the employees, the more likely its success. At the same time, the more clear the intent of the process, the more likely the employees, as they become associates, will think and act in the direction required by the executive for his dream and his organization.

Infiltration and Insinuation

The only part of Executive Thinking that is abundantly and consistently apparent is the dream that underlies everything the organization does. The dream is the consistent intent of everything to do with the organization. It is the basis for all actions taken—the cause—and relates directly to the outcomes achieved—the effect.

The executive must be vigilant in speaking his dream to the organization. The more public, the better. The more often, the better. The more graphic, the better. As noted earlier, the executive will be convinced that he has said enough about his dream—that everyone knows what he is looking for and will pursue it. He will be wrong.

The dream is new to everyone other than the executive. Even being privy to an executive's dream is new to the organization. How often is it that management and employees are informed about the goals and direction of executive management? Rarely. In most cases, strategic plans are locked away and purposely kept from the lower levels of executive and operational management. This is ostensibly done as a safety precaution protecting the proprietary direction and goals of the organization. In fact, it creates a rift in the organization where executives, managers, and

153

employees are left with the feeling that they are not trusted and with a lack of the information that would lead them to understand how they could be of greater benefit to the organization.

The executive must speak to his dream. He must not, however, speak to Executive Thinking as a process. This would lead to the misconception that Executive Thinking is just another program to be superimposed onto the organization. Instead, he must, without naming the process, speak to how the process works. Beginning with the ambassadors and the working ambassadors and leading to his announcements and pronouncements to the associates, he must speak to the importance of thinking as part of the organization. He must speak to how much is currently being lost from the organization by not accessing the thoughts of its members and how much will be gained through their involvement and engagement with the dream. This not only exposes the dream to the body of the organization, but also begins the process of establishing a shared ownership of the dream by the executive and his soon-to-be associates.

Infiltration begins with the dream. The executive is consistently and relentlessly verbal and outspoken about the dream. He incorporates it into everything that he, the ambassadors, and the working ambassadors communicate to the organization. The dream is the basis of the decisions being made and communicated, and they are communicated within the context of the dream and its outcomes. This ensures that the actions that are subsequently taken are in direct alignment with the executive's intent—the achievement of the dream.

Initially, employees—especially if they are invited to attend a meeting specifically for the purpose of the executive speaking to his dream—will be wary and will wonder what is really going on. The executive, in describing and discussing the dream, must position it as one that the employees must share. Their role and responsibility is to bring depth and breadth to the dream. They must be told and told again that their thinking—about their jobs, how those jobs are performed, and the actions that should be taken to ensure the accomplishment of the dream—is integral to the success of the dream. The dream will not be achieved and the organization will not succeed without the committed contribution of all employees to the dream's achievement and success.

It is for this reason and at this time that the executive makes it clear that the heretofore employees are now considered associates. They are associates of the organization and of the dream. It is through their contributions that the dream will be accomplished. The title is not given lightly. It is a sign of the collegiality, collaboration, and shared interests that are necessary to ensure the success of the dream.

As associates of the dream and of the organization, they are central figures. They are the tactical and operational arm of the organization. Though the executive may dream, the associates make the dream come true.

Eventually, as the dream continues to be discussed and used as an organizational context, it will begin to infiltrate the thinking of the associates. It is at this point, as they begin sharing the dream and shifting their thinking toward the dream, that they actually become associates. Until this time there may be those who scoff at the new title. Once the dream and the associates' part in that dream become manifest, that attitude will disappear.

The executive's early assessment of his organization is of primary importance at this time. He and his ambassadors have had numerous in-depth discussions about the organization, its complexity, the potential obstacles to the achievement of the dream, ad infinitum. It is at this point that the value of those discussions becomes apparent.

The executive assessment of the organization will be the basis upon which decisions will be made regarding exactly how to insinuate Executive Thinking into the organization. The challenge lies in promoting the concept and actions of thinking into a previously nonthinking organization.

This is not to say that thinking has not been going on until this time. Rather, the thinking that has been pursued has not been toward the intent and purpose of the organization. In part, this is a result of the lack of knowledge of that intent and purpose. In greater part, it is because the management of the organization has not presented thinking as a valued—and value-added—activity to the organization. This is not because management has considered thinking unimportant. It is because there has been an erroneous assumption that positive and purposeful thinking has been going on all along. That is, of course, not the case.

The executive assessment of the organization and its culture, in combination with the level and immediacy of need, will determine the process used to move Executive Thinking to the working ambassadors and the associates of the organization. These considerations must include the speed with which the dream needs to be implemented, the comfort and flexibility of the organization with speed and change, and the complexity of the organization in its structure and operations.

If the organization is at or near crisis, speed and flexibility are of paramount importance. In this case, there must be more than a sense of urgency. There must be an understanding that there is no longer any time for the organization to do anything other than change—and change immediately. Associates must accept that the organization cannot continue as it has to this point and that the alternative thoughts and actions of its employees not only must be spoken but also must be acted upon.

In such a case, it is the executive's responsibility to make unilateral decisions regarding what has to be done, and the dream, such as it will be until things settle down, is wholly nonnegotiable. Everyone's responsibility is to buy in and to act accordingly. Part of that buy-in and action is a quick and decisive generation of alternative ways of making the business work. Whether it is in terms of product quality and safety, cost efficiencies, or any aspect of organizational effectiveness, every associate's thoughts must be turned toward the crisis at hand.

Oddly, this creates a bond in most organizations that continues long after the crisis has been averted. In such situations, the executive and the organization operate as comrades in arms. There is a defined enemy—the demise of the organization—and it comes from outside the organization. The executive, as general, leads his troops—all of whom are now able to see the enemy for who and what that enemy is—toward success.

This is probably the only time that allusions to war rather than a dance are appropriate in the organization. Working in a concerted way against a known and defined external enemy in a cooperative effort provides a shared experience and a shared sense of accomplishment. There should not be a sense of fear established. Instead, there should be a sense of crisis, urgency, and importance to the situation and to the associates, who are the first and foremost line of defense against failure.

In most cases, organizations will not find themselves in current crisis. Rather they are operating in such a way that everyone is used to doing what they do, and even though the world outside of the organization is changing, everything inside is being maintained much as it has been in the past. In such cases, associates must become aware that if they do not change how they do what they do—if they do not enact and achieve the dream—they will no longer continue to exist as they have before. This sense of urgency is one that is positive for the organization. It is a directive force providing a justification for the alternative thinking that is to come.

The directive force in both the cases of actual and potential crisis differs in fact and in tone from establishing a sense of fear in the organization. The dream and the thinking necessary to achieve the dream are motivating forces. Fear, however, is a paralyzing force. The executive, in speaking to the need for change in the organization, must present a realistic picture of the present as a justification for the enhanced present and thriving future. The dream must not be positioned as a reaction to or as a reason for fear. The tone must be one of clear direction, success, and purpose.

If the organization is flexible in nature and in its historical operations, Executive Thinking will be more easily accepted and implemented. Flexibility results from a comfort with change. The executive, as he speaks his dream, must speak to the need for change as a positive force.

The structure and complexity of the organization as it exists will impact the decision about how best to insinuate Executive Thinking into the organization. The executive assessment will have identified unnecessary structural components and complexities. As implementation progresses, each of these will be systematically addressed.

The executive and ambassadors should take particular note of where, when, and how the organization does not work in a simple and elegant line. These organizational speed bumps are the ways by which employees in the past have protected the status quo. They slow and misdirect progress enough to knock it off course. The executive and ambassadors should pay particular heed to this pattern as it represents a majority of known obstacles the process will encounter. However, the more thorough the assessment and its application prior to implementation, the more those obstacles will be addressed and avoided both before and as Executive Thinking progresses.

The preferred mode of implementation is one of integration. Executive Thinking concepts and actions are integrated into the discussion at already existing staff and other meetings. Once again, Executive Thinking should not be presented as something everyone is now supposed to do. When implemented correctly, while everyone is aware that they are doing things differently, there is no sense of an imposed system or process to the changes being manifest. That is the hallmark of successful infiltration and integration of the process.

Executive Thinking, as it is manifest within the body of the organization, is a conscious application of new behaviors. The behaviors, however, look not so much like organizational behaviors as they do like human behaviors.

People take an interest in what others think. People are told why they are doing what they are doing. Questions are asked and answers are considered. Disagreements occur but are treated as positive discourse all for the same purpose—the achievement of the dream.

When the ambassadors or working ambassadors are speaking of the dream, they speak of it in operating terms. They speak to the goals of the organization and its strategy. They speak to what the overall organization is trying to achieve and how their particular part of the organization can assist in that achievement. They develop that sense of community that lends itself to shared purpose and shared excellence.

ℰ◉ℒ

Creating the Environment

In order for the organization to be primed to integrate and adopt Executive Thinking as a means of achieving the dream, the executive and her ambassadors must create the appropriate environment across the organization.

That environment must transcend the organization's structure and operations. It must be found in all locations and at all levels. It must become and remain the prime operational directive for the organization in all of its functional areas, locations, and operations.

There are three basic components of the environment. They are *commitment, interest,* and *action.* As with the rest of Executive Thinking, the organization's environment is based on a system of reciprocity. Opportunities are provided to the associates to be fully engaged in the future and ongoing success of the organization. That success is, to a great extent, dependent upon the associates' commitment to the organization and its dream. The associates, like the executive and her ambassadors, must take an active interest in the organization, its goals, and the contributions that are being made and can be further made by all of the associates. Each associate is an integral part of the dream. Finally, in order to ensure success, the dream and Executive Thinking must move from thought to action. The enterprise must be fully engaged in the manifestation of the breadth and depth of the dream.

Just as with the trust components, each environmental component must be present to ensure the appropriate environment for success. And, like trust, each is behaviorally based. The more often and consistently the executive and her ambassadors model the appropriate environmental behaviors, the more quickly the associates will adopt and reciprocate the behaviors. This reciprocity will be not only in the way associates treat one another and their management, but also in the ways they work to support the achievement of the dream.

Commitment

The dream of the executive acts as the intent of the organization and, as such, that to which the organization must be *committed.* To create a truly committed environment, the dream must be made and remain apparent in all discussions and in all actions taken throughout the enterprise.

The dream is the context of the organization. It is the dream to which each individual throughout the organization must be committed. The dream must be positioned so that its intent is clear and its outcomes are of benefit to everyone. In this way, it becomes more than just the dream of the executive. It becomes the dream of each and every associate throughout the organization.

The dream cannot be exclusive or exclusionary. Only by presenting the dream as an inclusive goal can the executive be assured that the individuals within the body of the organization will become committed. The achievement of the dream must insinuate itself into the personal and professional agendas of each individual.

One of the clearest ways to show commitment is for the executive and his ambassadors to allow for and approve of changes throughout the organization. Associates, in the form of employees, will believe that they have gone through such organizational change attempts before. In most of those cases, they will have been left with the feeling that while they may have been committed to the improvement of the organization, the management wasn't. This lack of management support was, to the employees, demonstrated by management's lack of consistency and apparent commitment to the stated goal.

By listening to the associates' input and allowing them to take action as and when appropriate, the executive and his ambassadors demonstrate their commitment to the real change of the organization. Environmentally this sends a crucial message throughout the enterprise. It says, "We are working toward the dream. We will do whatever is necessary to get there. We are committed to the dream and to everyone in the organization's ability to assist us in achieving that dream."

Over the long term, this also lays the groundwork for an innovative environment in the organization. By making change not only acceptable but preferred, and because changes have been made as a result of associate input toward the goal, the organization begins to be positioned for wholly alternative, new, and creative ideas. It is these ideas that will form the basis for the next level of the dream.

Commitment is demonstrated behaviorally through the consistent context of the dream and the consistent support for the associates in their attempts to achieve the dream. For long-term growth and expansion, these components must be in place. They create the basis for a safe environment—safe to try new ideas, suggest and implement new products or services, identify growth areas and new areas of opportunity.

The information and thinking that create immediate success as well as long-term innovation already exist within the organization. By creating a safe, committed environment, the organization can then access that thinking and information and develop it further. Those who want to be involved in this next level can be. Those who do not want to be involved don't have to be. Nonetheless, everyone within the organization benefits from the thoughts and innovations that are generated throughout the enterprise.

Interest

It begins with a question. It thrives because of the *interest* in the answer.

Executive Thinking and the achievement of the dream are dependent upon the creation of an interested and interesting organization. Too often, organizations as they languish become uninterested in anything but the task at hand. In an Executive Thinking organization, each individual is vitally interested in the enterprise. As well, each individual is vitally interested in the input and thoughts of the other associates at all levels and in all locations.

The most direct and visible means of showing interest and making Executive Thinking work throughout the organization is the dialogue process. Executive Thinking is a system based on discussion, understanding, and action. Ultimately, these are the components and outcomes of the dialogue process.

The underlying assumption is that the people engaged in the dialogue are interested in the input and thoughts of others. If they are not interested, there is no real dialogue and, as such, no possibility of Executive Thinking. If they are interested and that interest is demonstrated on a consistent basis, the dialogue—and Executive Thinking in general—becomes the operating procedure for the achievement of the dream.

The dialogue is the most insidious part of Executive Thinking. Without realizing it, associates throughout the organization at all levels are drawn into the dream and the thinking process. Their thoughts are requested. Interest in those thoughts is apparent. Actions based on the thoughts are discussed and taken. In the cause-effect model, the dialogue is the initial step of the manifestation of intent. The dream acts as the basis for the dialogue. The thoughts of the ambassadors and associates provide the basis for action. The alignment between cause and effect is assured.

The organization must also work to be an interesting enterprise. As the organization succeeds in its work toward the dream, it must attract the best and the brightest to ensure its ability to grow and develop in the current as well as in future dreams. Some of the best and the brightest will come from within the organization. Executive Thinking and other developmental processes will provide the opportunity and the direction for previously unknown internal talent to be discovered. That is all for the good. However, that internal development should also be augmented and enhanced through ongoing and—depending upon the industry and the enterprise's planned growth—sometimes aggressive attraction of outside talent.

Becoming an interesting organization also acts to support the executive's primary, external universe. As the organization becomes of greater interest, it will also experience a progressive and consistent growth in attention from investors, potential partners, and the like. This provides the executive with greater means of achieving his longer-term goals for the organization. It also assists in keeping the executive well balanced as he works within his two universes. The executive experiences support and success in both universes during and as a result of Executive Thinking.

Action

Executive Thinking and the thinking organization are most clearly identified by the penchant for *action* that pervades the enterprise. Each associate at every level and in every location knows that good ideas without associated actions are, ultimately, worthless. It is only those ideas that work toward the achievement of the dream and that are manifest in actions that have real value to the associates and to their organization.

The organization must be committed to action. An Executive Thinking organization is one that is flexible and fast moving. Change is a norm and it is preferred. The existence of the dream maintains the overall direction of the organization. At the same time, actions are being taken on a continuous and continual basis to manifest the dream. The actions, as intermediaries, are part of both the cause and the effect side of the model. Action is necessary for both to exist.

There is a common misconception that participative organizations are soft organizations. This misconception comes from the mismanagement of participative processes in manufacturing and service organizations across industries. Too often, participation has been used as an excuse for inaction. Too many people were involved in decision making, leading to no decisions and, ultimately, to no actions being taken.

Such mismanagement does not and cannot exist in an Executive Thinking organization. An organization committed to Executive Thinking is also committed to the actions necessary to achieve the dream. It is not a soft organization. It is a strong and purposeful organization. By establishing a dream that is shared by everyone, there is a constant ability and desire to monitor actions to ensure their alignment with the intended goal.

In an Executive Thinking organization, Deming's concern about the disconnect between intent and method is unnecessary. By using a cause and effect model for Executive Thinking, and by creating an environment within which everyone knows, understands, and is committed to the same goals, there can be no disconnect between intent and action. Misdirected action or inaction will immediately be identified and questioned. Tolerance for purposeful misdirection or inaction will not exist.

The environment of the organization is, by combining commitment, interest, and action, designed to ensure alignment and success. The goals set out by the executive in the form of the dream, and the extended dream as it is enhanced and augmented by the ambassadors and associates, ultimately become the overriding cause and effect. The organization is operating to the dream. By doing so, it is achieving the dream. A perfect circle is created. The dream becomes self-perpetuating and self-regenerating. The organization is positioned for ongoing and continuous success and growth.

ᏕᎧᎯ

The Empowerment Paradox

Once the executive has communicated the dream and everyone has begun the engagement process, the organization must look quickly to its empowerment process.

Empowerment is a crucial component of Executive Thinking and of the ability of the organization to achieve the dream. It also is one of the most perilous processes for the executive and presents some of the most difficult challenges the organization will encounter.

Empowerment is developmental. So is Executive Thinking. It is unsafe for the organization to unconditionally empower the associates before the executive and her ambassadors have some understanding of the associates' current and developing capabilities. It is necessary that an empowerment system be developed and implemented. However, prior to that occurring, the executive and her ambassadors must understand the paradox inherent in empowerment.

That paradox is that the stronger the executive and her direction and management of the organization, the more empowered the associates can be. In effect, the more paternalistic the organization, the more freeing for its associates.

This seems like a contradiction in terms. Empowerment, as it is understood, is the movement of decision-making authority to lower levels of management and employees. Normally it is thought that the only way in which employees can be empowered is by management giving up its authority to make decisions. A strong management and direction of the organization, then, would seemingly lead to a powerless employee base.

In fact, the stronger the direction and management, the more able the associates are to take on the necessary empowerment and use their decision-making authority wisely. The direction—in this case in the form of the dream and as manifest in the dialogue—creates the parameters for empowerment. As the associates develop their understanding of the dream and of how their job affects and is affected by the dream, and actively begin working toward the achievement of the dream, the systematic empowerment of the organization is not only possible but preferable.

Too often employees are endowed with empowerment before they are equipped to handle it or use it appropriately. This is usually because the employees do not understand the goals and direction of the organization. As a result, the empowerment process provides great opportunity for the employees to unknowingly undermine the real intent of the organization.

In the case of Executive Thinking, this cannot be the case. Throughout the process, the executive and her ambassadors are assessing and reassessing the dream and its progress throughout the organization. Each ambassador is working with his functional areas to determine needs for additional information or other needs. As these needs are identified—and particularly as the information needs lessen because of increased knowledge base—the associates are continually being groomed for more and greater responsibility and authority.

This is not to say that management in the form of the working ambassadors, ambassadors, or executive loses its decision-making authority and responsibility. On the contrary. The decisions made by the associates as the empowerment process and Executive Thinking progress are a direct reflection of the decision-making authority of the management of the area. It is the responsibility of the executive and management to ensure that the decisions of the associates are the best-informed decisions. In effect, the decisions of the associates should be exactly those that the executive or ambassador would have made had she had the same information with which to work.

At no time can the executive step back or away from her management responsibility to the organization. She is the leader. She is looked to for direction and guidance. She is also monitored by the associates for her modeling of supportive behaviors. This does not mean, however, that she or her ambassadors should be the ones making all of the decisions.

The organization as a reflection of the executive and her ambassadors—particularly as Executive Thinking extends and expands throughout the enterprise—will be an organization of strong and directed decision making. It will not waffle. The person or people most closely responsible for an area or task responsibility will make decisions as and when needed. While information will flow, it should not be filtered before decisions can be made. The empowerment system allows the cleanest, clearest decisions to be made because those decisions are being made by the people who have the best and most immediate information about the issue.

If bad decisions are being made in any part of the organization, it is the responsibility of the executive and her ambassadors to find out why. In most cases, it is because of an information breakdown between the executive, the ambassador, and the decision-making area. In some cases, it is due to inconsistencies being communicated by the management of the area. These inconsistencies lead to misunderstanding by the associates about what they can or should be doing. In such cases, rather than the associates making clear and directed decisions, their decisions are based on a second-guessing process. That process takes nearly blind shots at what the associates believe management wants—this time.

Organizations are hierarchical. Hierarchy is paternalistic. Therefore, organizations—no matter how simple or complex—are paternalistic. From the associates' perspective, that hierarchical, paternalistic relationship provides both safety and a hiding place. The safety is in the checks and balances the structure provides. Associates can ask their immediate management for clarification prior to making decisions or taking action. There is a sense of camaraderie and collegiality to the process that makes it perceptibly safer and more enjoyable for the associates.

When used inappropriately, the associates use the hierarchy as a hiding place. Sometimes this is the place of victims. The victims use the hierarchy as a finger-pointing target that neatly sets management out as the reason things cannot be done. More often, employees not engaged in the development and success of the organization use the hierarchy as a means of abdicating decision-making responsibility. For them it is far more comfortable to remove themselves from the decision-making responsibilities that might ultimately lead to accountability. These employees are not victims. They are scared.

As part of the paternalistic structure, the executive and her ambassadors must understand that they have a comparably parental role as they work to develop the associates and achieve the dream. To as great an extent as possible, the executive and her ambassadors must model the appropriate behaviors, provide the greatest learning opportunities, be teachers and mentors, and hold the associates responsible and accountable for their actions so that their learning is experiential. In so doing, the executive and ambassadors are freeing the associates to fly on their own. Through the direction and oversight the executives and ambassadors provide, they are grooming the associates for greater accomplishments that they will be able to make on their own.

The greater the investment of time at the beginning of the process, the freer the associates will be as the process progresses. Moreover, the greater that investment, the sooner the executive and ambassadors will be able to step back and allow the organization to extend and expand itself in the achievement of the dream. This will then free the executive to develop her next dream.

By understanding and operating to the paradox inherent in empowerment, the executive creates the appropriate environment for the successful achievement of the dream. The intent is always clear—the dream is to be realized. The implementation of a developmental empowerment system causes the intent to be achieved. Once again, the cause-effect circle is complete.

✲

Understanding and Managing the White Space

One of the more popular organizational buzz phrases has been for management to "manage the white space." The concept is apt. Rather than thinking of the organization as a vertical or horizontal model based on the organization chart, management should look at the organization and act upon it based on the undrawn relationships within and between departments, divisions, functions, levels, and locations.

The white space of the organization describes how the organization really works. While the organization chart describes the formal functional relationships, the white space describes the informal operational relationships. People do not operate the way the organization is structured—even if the rules and regulations to do so are concrete. Organizations are relationship based. People relate to other people as and whenever necessary. Contrary to how the organization is structured to operate, in actuality it operates based on those contacts and relationships—all of which exist in and make up the white space.

The drawn lines of the organization represent the formal policies, procedures, and practices. The white space represents the informal behind-the-scenes dealings that take place at every level to get things done. It is not that the participants are intentionally breaking the rules. It is that they are working as close to the rules as they can—knowing that they are pushing the envelope—to achieve what they understand to be the goals of the organization.

In order for the dream of the executive to succeed, it must exist functionally using the structure and rules and, more important, thrive in the white space of the organization. The ability of the dream to transcend the organization's structure is a hallmark of its success. Executive Thinking is a relationship-based process using dialogue as its method of developing contacts and relationships. As a result, it exists in the white space and assists the organization and its executive in making best use of that transcendent structure.

The most direct method of accomplishing this goal is to create a consistent environment based on the three environmental components throughout the organization. While it is understood and necessary that each location or function will have to adapt the environment to suit its needs and operating requirements—as well as the societal requirements for multinational organizations—the components of the environment should be recognizable throughout the enterprise.

༄༅

Executive Thinking and Organizational Alignment

The ultimate cause-effect outcome is in the establishment of alignment throughout the organization. As stated from the first, for employees at all levels to truly be associates of the enterprise, they must know what to think about. They must have clarity and direction in all of their actions. They must know what the organization is trying to achieve and why. Then they must apply their thinking skills to determining how their function and they themselves can assist and assure the organization in achieving the goals set out for it.

Organizational alignment moves Executive Thinking out of the boundaries of any particular functional area and creates a united whole consisting of the entire enterprise.

Each function must know how it fits into the organizational structure and purpose. Questions must be asked about formal and informal relationships throughout the organization.

One of the most common problems encountered by organizations is the lack of understanding of how the actions of one function affect another. There is a tendency for associates, particularly as they begin the thinking process, to think first and only in terms of their own function. When they incorporate other functions into their discussions, the context is usually how those other functions are not supporting their needs. To a certain extent this is normal and to be expected. The initial discussions will sound far more like venting than like productive, directed dialogue.

From the first, however, the discussion must be moved toward the interactive effects of the functions. Alignment is the creation of a simple and elegant line across and throughout the organization. The line begins with the executive and his dream at one end. At the other end is the operational manifestation of the dream in each and every function. Ultimately, there is no beginning and no end. What started out as two ends becomes one inextricably bound entity that reflects the dream in every action taken throughout the enterprise.

This type and level of understanding must be pursued from the first. As the associates discuss the ways by which they and their function can assist in achieving the goal, the impact and interaction of other functions must be considered. This is the conscious and purposeful operationalization of the white space.

Remember that the discussion will be using the executive triumvirate as the basis of thought. As the associates think like executives—chief executive, chief operating, and chief financial officers—they must take on a more global, less limited view. Executive Thinking is interactive thinking. Interactive thinking leads to an understanding and manifestation of alignment throughout the organization.

Alignment must be discussed in real terms in every function. As the dream is continually insinuated into the thinking and actions of the associates, the ways by which alliances can be built within and between functions must also be discussed. The easiest way to achieve this goal is through information sharing.

During the dialogue process, questions will undoubtedly be asked about how a particular area can work more proactively and productively with another. These questions will usually occur as a result of the identification of an obstacle to the achievement of the dream. Blame is not assessed and fingers are not pointed. It is simply understood that there are more people involved than just the one area. This makes it both necessary and sensible to create an alliance with that other area—and with progressively more areas after that.

The ambassador must ensure that the associates remember there is only one side—the side of the organization. Further, no matter how, each and every associate is working to the same goal—the achievement of the dream.

The establishment and creation of alliances and, ultimately, of alignment provide the greatest opportunity for the associates to understand the steps of the dance. No matter at what level or in what function, each associate must learn to move upward, downward, and outward in concert with the other associates and functions. As each function begins to dance with its associate functions, the ballroom becomes filled with dancers who all know the steps, hear the same music, and move as one.

This is an Executive Thinking organization. Everyone in every part of the organization understands how his part of the organization fits into the greater whole. The associates, by this time, are seeing the results of their thinking and actions. They have been asked to think like executives and they are doing so. They are providing greater input with more depth and understanding. They are actively working with their colleagues within and outside of their function to ensure the greater good. They are engaged with and in the dream.

Each individual sees the dream as his dream—something to which he is now and will remain committed. He knows that the dream achieves not only the organization's goals, but also his own goals. He is learning and growing each and every day. Work has become not just a place to be, but a place he wants to be.

E X E C U T I V E   T H O U G H T S

By viewing the laws of cause and effect prior to and throughout the implementation process, the organization is positioned—and continues to position itself—for success. Executive Thinking, as an active process based on the dream of the executive, is both a catalyst and an outcome toward success.

The dream is the context of the organization. It is the dream to which each individual throughout the organization must be committed. The dream must be positioned so that its intent is clear and its outcomes are of benefit to everyone. In this way, it becomes more than just the dream of the executive. It becomes the dream of each and every associate throughout the organization.

The paradox of empowerment is that the stronger the executive and his direction and management of the organization, the more empowered the associates can be. In effect, the more paternalistic the organization, the more freeing for its associates. In fact, the stronger the direction and management, the more able the associates are to take on the necessary empowerment and use their decision-making authority wisely.

178

CHAPTER 8

COMMITMENTS

AN EXECUTIVE THINKING ORGANIZATION
is one that is committed to a long-term Vision For the
organization—the dream—in combination with immediate and ongoing actions taken to support, manifest, and
exceed that dream. It is also an organization committed to
a system of reciprocity. Each individual within the enterprise must know her responsibilities and be held accountable for them. In turn, each individual must hold her colleagues and co-workers responsible for their part in the
enterprise. This is the basis for trust. At the most global
level, the executive must ensure that the organization is

structurally and functionally designed and managed to consistently support only those behaviors that are in support of the organization.

The only way that all of these commitments can be kept is for the specific behavioral expectations within the organization to be delineated and modeled. Building an organization that is designed for long-term product and service success cannot be accomplished unless there is a complementary culture in the organization. This culture is based on the defined and manifest expectations and commitments to and within the enterprise. The ways and means of the organization—not just the tasks, but the human operations of the organization—must be as clearly laid out as if they were operating procedures or instructions.

The expectations of and for each individual must be identified, defined, disseminated, and modeled. Those same expectations must be managed by the executive, ambassadors, and working ambassadors. Once the expectations have been communicated, it is incumbent upon each individual to ensure that she conforms to those expectations. This creates a human environment within the organization that allows and supports the operational environment's ability to succeed.

Some of the behaviors requested and demanded of the associates may seem imposed, particularly at first. They also may seem noticeably different to those customers who first come into contact with the organization. Quickly, however, they set a tone that is adopted and expected by both the associates and the customers. It is a respectful tone that acknowledges the right of every individual to be treated as a valued human being. It is this tone that sets the organization apart and enables it and its associates to move to its next levels of success.

Whether internally or externally, these expectations and commitments are not to be confused with "customer service." Customer service is but a small component of the expectations that must be incorporated into the organization. It is not just a matter of being polite. It is the commitment to excel. It is the commitment to one's associates and one's customers that everything that can be done will be done to ensure a mutual success.

Granted, these expectations and commitments manifest themselves in polite, respectful behaviors. However, by looking beneath the surface it becomes immediately apparent that there is far more to the behavior than just the outward manifestations. In such cases, these associates are not just going through the motions.

A fascinating example of how the behaviors are underlaid by much greater expectations and commitments took place in one of the restaurants at the San Francisco Ritz-Carlton Hotel. What have come to be the expected Ritz-Carlton behaviors were in evidence. The response to "thank you" was "my pleasure." Before being asked, the waiter provided everything that could have been desired. It was a typically excellent Ritz-Carlton dining experience.

The fascination occurred after the meal. On departing the restaurant, it was observed that a group of serving personnel from the restaurant had surrounded the waiter who had provided the service. The other personnel were asking the waiter where he had learned how to say and do certain things that they had noted. They asked him to explain how he did them and what phrases, exactly, he had used. They subsequently repeated the phrases to him to make sure that they were saying them correctly.

The waiter was neither a trainer nor a team leader. He was a colleague who had been noted by his associates as being able to provide even greater service and attention than they themselves considered that they were providing. The conversation among the associates occurred after the restaurant was closed. The service personnel were taking their own time asking this waiter for his guidance. They not only wanted to learn, they also acknowledged his excellence in the process. Even more fascinating was that each of the service personnel treated the after-hours conversation as if it were something normal and in no way out of the ordinary. This, more than anything, demonstrated the extent to which the organization had integrated into its environment the expectations and commitments desired and deserved by both the associates and the customers.

It is easy to say that of course one would find such behaviors being demonstrated by an organization such as the Ritz-Carlton. It is an international, award-winning hotel chain that differentiates itself through its levels of service. Such behaviors would only be expected. Others would not be tolerated.

While this is arguably correct, the real lesson in this example is not the service provided to the customers. That is to be expected. The far more compelling lesson is the commitment of the associates to their own task and their excellence in performing that task. They know what the expectations are for them and of and for the organization. Through their commitment to achieving those goals, they extend themselves in a noncompetitive way, actively learning and benefiting from each other. Ultimately it is the associates, the organization, and the customers who all benefit from that commitment.

Another example of the demonstration of these behaviors occurs in a radically different organization. It is the Chevron Oil-Stop. The Chevron Oil-Stop is a quick-serve, drive-through automobile repair and maintenance service. It is in direct competition with other such entities that have been in the market for a longer time and have much greater name recognition and visibility in the marketplace.

The Oil-Stop, however, differentiates itself through the behaviors of its associates toward their colleagues as well as their customers. For the customer, the outcome is much the same as from other such providers. One drives in for an oil change or other maintenance and drives out again a few minutes later with the work completed.

The experience during the course of that maintenance process, however, is vastly different from that which can be expected at other providers. The customer is greeted and offered a beverage to partake of during the maintenance and while staying in his car. Customers are always treated politely and called by their last name. Any time an associate approaches the customer with a comment or question, the customer is always acknowledged by name. Uniforms are neat and pressed, and the work area is clean and tidy.

For the associates during the process, the treatment of their colleagues is respectful and consistently acknowledging. As they call out requests or questions to one another, they behave with an almost military politeness. Each associate acknowledges requests from another with a response of either yes or no, sir (or ma'am). Thank you is a phrase that is in evidence throughout the process as the associates acknowledge responses or services provided by their colleagues. There is no time during which the associates, who are calling loudly to one another to combat the noise in the work area, raise their voices in anything other than a positive and respectful acknowledgment of their own or their associates' efforts.

For the customer, this creates an environment that instills trust in the associates and in their organization. There is a sense of thoroughness that is implied by the associates' behaviors. For the associates, the environment is one in which they are required to consistently acknowledge their own and each other's contributions. The behavioral expectations are very clear. These translate to a demonstrated commitment among and between associates to the goals of the operation.

No matter at what level or in what type of organization, the more and better the expectations and commitments are laid out, the more likely the organization is to succeed. These behaviors, which must be reciprocal, lead the organization to a level of performance not previously experienced. That level of performance is achievable and can be maintained because each associate knows what is expected of her, as well as what the benefit will be to her and to the organization as a whole.

Expectations, Tolerance, and the Executive Thinking Organization

Expectations and commitments play a very important role in the development of the associates in their role as executive thinkers. It is not by accident that executives get things done. It is by conscious thought, action, and follow-up that they ensure not only that their part of the action is taken, but also that any other complementary actions are also completed. Executives are vigilant in making sure that their ideas are implemented. As the organization expands and extends itself using Executive Thinking, the associates also must take on this vigilant behavior system. They must be as relentless as their executive in ensuring that actions are taken, that no time or energy is lost, and that everything is working toward the achievement of the dream.

One of the problems that might well be encountered is the mistaken impression that a participative organization is a tolerant organization. This is and must be patently untrue. There can be no tolerance for behaviors that are not in keeping with the goals, expectations, and commitments of the organization to its associates and to its stakeholders.

Organizations and their management have become far too tolerant of aberrant behaviors. It is not acceptable that timelines slip because of bad planning or execution. It is not acceptable that shoddy or incomplete products or services are released just to make the ship date. It is not acceptable that employees who do not work well in the organization are transferred and often promoted rather than either being developed or let go. It is not acceptable that performance appraisals are either not completed or not completed honestly. It is not fair to the organization or to its stakeholders.

Further, acceptance of such aberrant behaviors has established a rift within organizations between those associates who really are working to their potential and to the good of the organization and their management—whom they view as not supporting them by not dealing with the product, service, operations, or human resource issues of the organization. Dissatisfaction and low morale result. Movement out of the organization by valued employees becomes a norm. Ultimately, the organization, through its tolerance, is made up of those managers and employees who do the least work.

Most of this is invisible to the executive. She knows that the numbers do not reflect her expectations regarding profit or performance. She does not know why. Depending upon how closely she monitors the organization's operations—and until this time, she has spent little time doing so—she does not understand why or how that disconnect has come to be.

This is exactly the opposite of what should be happening within the enterprise. In an organization working to its potential, the best of every associate is consistently being demanded, accessed, and utilized. Rather than the best and the brightest leaving the organization, it is the best and the brightest who stay. Those who choose not to extend themselves and work to their highest potential find that the environment does not support their laissez-faire attitude. Either they get into alignment with the enterprise by working assiduously with their associates to achieve the dream, or they leave—and they do so of their own volition. People do not stay where they are actively unhappy or dissatisfied. If the organization passes them by, they will, in most cases, leave on their own to find an organization that better suits their values and working preferences.

To achieve the organization of her dreams, the executive must set, demand, and monitor expectations of excellence. She must model those behaviors and ensure that her ambassadors are modeling the same. She must be vigilant in her intolerance for anything less than excellence and constantly review the ways by which the organization is working to ensure that excellence is the norm.

౭☙

Expectations, Commitments, and Professionalism

No matter what the position, no matter what the responsibility, the greatest and most consistent expectation is professionalism. Professionalism is an expectation of the associate for herself and from the organization. It is also a commitment by the associate to herself and to the organization.

Think back to the custodian interviewed during the race to the moon. It didn't matter that organizationally he was at the lowest level of the hierarchy. It didn't matter that he wasn't part of the technical genius that would put a man on the moon. All that mattered was that he viewed his position as being of just as great importance as that of anyone else in the organization. He had responsibilities to his job and to the goals of the enterprise. His commitment was to fulfill those responsibilities and assist in accomplishing those goals. These are the hallmarks of a professional.

Everyone within the enterprise must view herself and be viewed by others as a professional. By doing so, the respectful behaviors accorded to professionals will then be justifiably applied. Every position and every person deserves that respect. This creates an understanding of the complementary needs of the organization—that the enterprise cannot succeed unless everyone and everything in the enterprise is committed to and working toward that success.

Professionalism demands a great deal from each associate. Each individual must be committed to doing the best she can to fulfill her responsibilities. This includes an ongoing analysis of how she is doing what she is doing. Further, it requires that she assess whether what she is doing and how fully addresses the needs of the enterprise and her role within the organization.

Professionalism also requires that each individual work toward her own development. She must be committed to her own ongoing learning as well as to the application of that learning. In order to stay competitive and to keep the organization competitive, she must commit to taking advantage of learning opportunities afforded by the organization.

More important, she must commit to finding and taking advantage of learning opportunities on her own—including those not paid for by the organization.

Professionalism is a personal trait that carries over into organizational behaviors. When an individual views herself as a professional, she immediately promotes herself to a higher level of operation and capability. The expectations of and for a professional are high. Professionals are highly qualified individuals. Without being pompous or arrogant about their capabilities, they know their value to the enterprise. They know that what they bring may be offered by others, but never in the same way and with the same level of greatness.

This is not said lightly. Individuals must view themselves with honor and integrity and then bring that honor and integrity to everything they do. The organization, through its environment and its operations, must do everything it can to support and enhance those traits. When the organization assists the individuals in achieving greatness, the organization achieves its own greatness at the same time.

The greatest power of Executive Thinking, starting with the executive and moving throughout the organization, is that it is based on the belief that there is greatness, value, and professionalism within every associate throughout the organization. It is a system designed to get the best from each individual. In so doing, it not only benefits the organization and its stakeholders but, possibly more important, it benefits each human affiliated internally and externally with the enterprise. Ultimately, greatness breeds greatness.

Setting and Raising Expectations

The expectations throughout the enterprise are based on the values of the executive as they are known and understood by the associates. The executive must make it abundantly and consistently clear that only the best will be expected and accepted from everyone. He must then, working with his ambassadors on an ongoing basis throughout the process, ensure that everything possible within the organization is being done to support the associates. No stone must be left unturned in the training and development, the management systems, or the operational improvements that will allow the associates to excel.

This commitment on the part of the organization to the associates demonstrates the reciprocity of the organization toward those who help it succeed. Associates cannot accomplish the dream on their own. They need the executive and his demonstrated support throughout the organization in order to achieve his dream and the shared goals for the present and for the future.

The values that must underlie this support, on the part of both the organization and its associates, are responsibility and accountability. Each functional entity within the organization must have clear responsibilities assigned to it. These must be known and understood by the associates who work within that function. There must be a sense and a pride of ownership felt by the associates toward their responsibilities.

Further, they must be held accountable for their actions within their own function and in working with other functions. Because the organization is committed to excellence across all areas and operations, each associate is responsible for assisting in ensuring that every action has a positive outcome not only in her own area but also in other areas that her area affects. Each action taken by any associate must be in keeping with the larger goals and dream of the enterprise.

From a historical perspective, responsibility and accountability have gained nearly a bad name in many organizations. As the tolerance for aberrant behaviors within organizations has grown, so, too, has the lackadaisical attitude toward responsibility and accountability. There is a tendency among employees to believe that they neither can nor should be held responsible or accountable for their actions. Sometimes this is based on their belief that they are victims of the system because they feel powerless. Sometimes it is a simple abdication and avoidance of going beyond what has been asked to this point.

This puts the onus on the executive and his ambassadors to ensure that each associate knows that what has been accepted before is no longer enough. It is not that the associates have not done a good job. It is that the job they have done is no longer adequate for the challenges of the present and those that lie ahead.

This raising of organizational expectations must be insinuated into the organization along with the rest of Executive Thinking. In the dialogue it begins by discussing what is already known to the associates. It progresses by examining that which was considered impossible. It becomes integrated by regular and rational discussion of what had previously been unimaginable.

This progression is a natural outgrowth of Executive Thinking as it grows and is adopted within the organization. Greater and expanded thinking leads to greater and expanded thoughts and actions. The first challenge is for the executive and his ambassadors to ensure that the value of such always rising expectations is known and understood. The associated challenge is for the executive to structure, operationalize, and prepare himself and the organization for a level of thinking, action, and responsiveness that had previously been unthinkable.

The executive must implant his expectations and values into every corner of the organization. Each associate must know that she cannot be committed only to her own agenda but must be committed to the agenda of the organization. That commitment must be demonstrated through the associate's active involvement not only in her own job but also in the increased productivity, efficiency, and effectiveness of others throughout the organization. Nothing less will be considered acceptable. Each associate's commitment, responsibility, and accountability are to the larger organization.

In contrast, yet in support of these values, there must be consequences for those employees who do not perform to the expectations and requirements of the organization. This presents one of the greatest interim transition challenges as the organization integrates Executive Thinking. In most organizations, no one is used to consequences any longer. Rarely are employees disciplined, and even more rarely are employees terminated from the organization. This is not to say that this should be the intent or *raison d'être* of management. On the contrary. The purpose of Executive Thinking is to get the most from everybody in the organization. Losing associates is not simply a loss of personnel, but a loss of their knowledge and understanding of the organization. That knowledge and understanding is invaluable and in many ways irreplaceable.

However, if there are no consequences there will be no possibility of long-term success for the organization—at least not to the level that could have been achieved. Those associates who dedicate themselves to the achievement of the dream must know that the organization is designed and operated to support them in that endeavor. In part this is realized by their ability to see that the organization will no longer tolerate conscious disrespect or intentional inaction toward the achievement of the dream.

Too often individuals dedicated to the enterprise leave because they are almost punished for their dedication. Managers quickly learn upon which individuals they can depend. For those dedicated employees, the reward is an increased workload and an ever-expanding task list. Concurrently they see their co-workers who are not dedicated, who do not work to the goals of the enterprise, being allowed to languish—sometimes while collecting a comparable or larger salary than the supposedly "valued" employee. For those valued employees, there is no value to them in staying.

If the co-workers are languishing because they are not adequately trained, then the onus is on management to ensure that appropriate training is provided. If they are languishing because their skill set does not lend itself to the tasks assigned, then it is the responsibility of that associate and her manager to identify where within the enterprise her skills can be put to use.

If, however, the employee is languishing because she has learned that she can and has no great desire to change that state of affairs, then the onus is on management to ensure that that employee learns that the state of affairs has changed around her. As an associate, she must be given every opportunity to excel within the organization. The need for her contribution and the desire for her active participation must be communicated to her. She must be given every opportunity to succeed.

Should she choose not to take advantage of that opportunity, the organization cannot afford to allow her to stay. The negative impact of her ongoing association with the enterprise is far too costly to the other associates, the working ambassador, and, ultimately, the dream. That associate is making her decision. She must take the consequences.

This demonstrated lack of tolerance for aberrant behaviors raises the professionalism of every other associate within the enterprise. For those associates who were and remain committed to the dream, the intolerance of irresponsibility equates to a recognition of those who take responsibility for their own part of the dream. In an unspoken and contrary way, it is an acknowledgment of those who are working with the executive toward his dream for their support.

Quantification and Results Thinking

One of the best and most straightforward ways in which expectations and achievement can be assessed on an ongoing basis is by quantifying progress toward the goal. Every organization has measurements. For the executive these measurements are usually and appropriately global. The question is, however, how representative are the measurements at any level of the organization?

An executive of a computer hardware manufacturing and distribution firm, in speaking with his management group, said, "I know we have data. We are drowning in data. The problem is that the data don't tell us anything—or at least not anything we can figure out." This is too often the case within the organization. Measurement systems abound. They simply don't either represent much of what is actually going on or address what needs to be known.

It is incumbent upon the associates and their working ambassadors to determine what they need to know and what they need to report about their particular function. This process must include and be based on objective measurement systems. The associates must have data to assess their own progress. Further, they need data to be able to create and present compelling arguments for the changes they wish to make.

Executive Thinking, because it is based on the cause-effect model, requires quantification. Associates must be able to assess, on a real-time and ongoing basis, whether their actions are, in fact, moving in the direction of the

195

dream. If so, they continue. If not, they have adequate forewarning that they are moving in an inappropriate direction. This gives them the ability to quickly change course through further analysis of where they went wrong and what they need to do about it.

Quantification also allows the ambassadors and working ambassadors to more comfortably implement the empowerment system. Measurement acts as part of the checks and balances system that makes it safe to expand the decision-making authority of the associates. As long as there are appropriate and up-to-date data, management can comfortably stand away from certain decisions and allow the associates to stretch their wings.

Further, because Executive Thinking is based on thinking that leads to action, the existence of a quantification system forces the organization to think in terms of action and outcomes. If the ambassadors and associates are not careful, they will find that it is too easy to unintentionally languish within the discussion and dialogue process.

Thinking is seductive. Once an idea is presented and discussion ensues, there is a tendency to want to stay with that idea until there is nothing left to discuss. If the participants are good at the dialogue, one idea will lead to another and then to another. While all of this thinking is good, it is not, ultimately, working toward the goals of the organization.

The dream can be achieved only through the actions of the associates. Granted, those actions are based on the original thinking. However, the actions are what lead to the manifest results.

Quantification of the process and progress toward the dream ensures that action occurs. It is a concrete, identifiable mile marker that clearly shows what has been achieved as well as what has yet to be achieved. It is a part of the Vision For the organization because it delineates how the organization is doing in its present and toward its future.

Executive Thinking is a balance between action and results. Problems occur only when and if the process is wholly biased toward one or the other. Action must occur in the form of thinking and the actions that ensue as a result of that thinking. Results occur based on the thinking and actions taken.

These may seem to be the same thing. They are not, however. The organization can find itself wholly focused on actions and not achieving the results it requires. Great thinking may occur and many actions may be taken. However, if that thinking and those actions are not taken in the context of the necessary results—the work toward the achievement of the dream—they run the risk of being merely action for action's sake.

Conversely, the organization can find itself wholly focused on results. This, in its way, is just as dangerous. Any organization can achieve anything it sets out to do. The question is, at what cost? If the thinking is wholly focused on results without any consideration for how those results are achieved, the organization runs great risk that it will not be able to maintain its achievements. Further, it runs the risk that the achievements will have come at such a great cost that the organization cannot continue in its present form or, possibly, in any form at all.

In all of these cases—whether the focus is exclusively on action or on results—the organization suffers because it has not adequately incorporated its goals with its means of monitoring and measurement. Expectations are not clear and the actions taken reflect that confusion. From the time the executive speaks to her dream, she must make clear that the ends and the means must complement each other.

One organization, a software development firm specializing in custom programs for corporate clients, nearly put itself out of business because of just this misunderstanding. A large, long-standing, and very lucrative client approached one of the vice presidents of development. The request by the client was to develop a program that would not only act as a bridge between previously designed programs, but also incorporate capabilities so that other software not designed by the same firm would be able to communicate using, in effect, one voice.

The vice president, in looking at his department's numbers, saw this opportunity not only as a means of ensuring that his department would reach its goals, but also as a way to potentially realize a substantially higher profit for the organization as a whole. His view was one of results. He knew that a project of this size and scope could mean the difference for the organization and, potentially, for his career.

Based on that analysis, he went ahead with the project. Without discussing the project requirements, but presenting the expected results to his senior executive, he actively lobbied for the organization to accept the project.

Even before the agreement was signed, he began assigning his designers responsibilities on the project, at the same time telling them that whatever priorities they had were to be made secondary. He remained committed and wanted his designers to be committed to the other projects. However, by his reckoning—a reckoning based on expected results only—the far more lucrative and valuable project was the new one.

It soon became apparent that there was more to the project than was originally thought. This was brought out in an executive meeting during which the vice president asked, "What do you do if you have a project that could make a big difference for the company but, if we do it, would cost the company so much it made us go bankrupt?" He was serious. From his perspective—a results perspective—the risk was not only worth it, it was expected.

Upon being questioned further, he admitted that the project was far more than his department or, in fact, the whole organization could do on its own. He even questioned exactly why the customer wanted the program designed. Ultimately, as these issues were brought out, the executive group determined that the project needed to be reassessed with an eye toward redesign and possible alliances with other organizations.

Eventually, the discussion turned toward how the vice president had come to the conclusion that this was a project that the organization should take on in the first place. As that discussion ensued, it became clear that the vice president believed that the whole and complete agenda of the senior executive was one of results. He believed that the senior executive was never concerned with what it would take to achieve the results—only that the organization got the jobs and completed them.

An analysis of the ways by which all of the vice presidents were measured and the measurements by which they assessed their areas found that all of the measurement systems being used were results indicators. The measurements were a reflection of the bias toward results across the organization. There were no process or progress measures. There were no interim or transitional measures. All measurements were either collected or reported on a monthly, quarterly, or by-project completion basis. In many cases, the measurements contradicted one another. Time-based measurements did not correlate with by-project measurements. Until the analysis was performed, however, because everyone was so used to seeing those measures, they did not realize how little valuable information they gained from those reports, or the extent to which their decision-making methods were being biased as a result of those measures.

As part of Executive Thinking, ambassadors, working ambassadors, and associates must actively assess how they view and how they measure what they do. The measures must reflect the totality of the enterprise, both in its actions and in its results. Further those measures must also provide insight into how the organization is doing toward its achievement of the dream. Overall, the combined measures must contain and reflect the necessary and complementary view of how the organization operates—one that balances action, results, and the progress toward the dream.

As part of that assessment, there must be an analysis of how the organization is measured and how the reward and recognition system is designed. One of the greatest operational challenges in an Executive Thinking organization is to ensure the alignment of the reward and recognition system with the direction and actions of the organization and its associates. At the best of times, reward and recognition is a challenge. In an Executive Thinking organization, particularly as the organization is transitioning in that direction, the challenge is even greater.

Reward and recognition is based on the premise that what is offered as a reward is of value to the associates. This is where problems most commonly occur. In most cases, associates do not view the reward as being of much value. Monetary rewards are usually greeted with the question, "Why is it so little?" Nonmonetary rewards are too often corporate gifts that are useful but not valuable to the receiver.

The intent of the reward and recognition system is to create an environment wherein individuals are acknowledged for their contribution to the enterprise. They are singled out as having achieved something of great value and something from which the organization and all of its stakeholders will benefit.

In an Executive Thinking organization, this is a particular challenge. Some of the greatest contributions to the organization are thoughts. These thoughts may be implemented by another group or function within the enterprise. The thoughts, even though they arose from one individual, were undoubtedly built upon by any number of associates before they resulted in the contribution being recognized.

Executive Thinking organizations bring participation to a new level. The reward and recognition system, therefore, must be designed to enhance and augment that participative process. Particularly where reward is involved, it cannot be exclusionary. It must be designed to incorporate and recognize all those who have had a part in the achievement. The system must be based on achievement toward the dream. There must be a direct, identified, and quantified correlation between the contribution and the dream. Further, this correlation should be apparent to all of the associates.

The safest monetary reward mechanism in an Executive Thinking organization is one that is organizationwide. Whether through profit sharing or gain sharing, if all of the associates benefit equally from everybody's contributions, the competitive and potentially warlike aftermath of conventional reward systems will be avoided. Additional monetary gain systems, such as employee stock ownership programs, matched contribution retirement programs, and the like, should also be available to the associates. These, while not part of the formal reward system, act as a reward for being an associate of the organization.

Eventually, as the organization achieves the dream and its profit-making outcomes, the formalized reward system will provide a much greater payout to the associates. This is the ultimate monetary reward for the associates' contributions. It is visible to and understood by the associates as being a result of their efforts. Ultimately, this will act as a financial spur in concert with their other levels of satisfaction, leading them to remain committed as the dream is expanded.

This also makes it easier for the organization to adopt an individual or function-based nonmonetary recognition system designed to give particularly deserved kudos to exceptional contributors. Even in those cases, the recognition system should be designed to ensure that the contributors who receive recognition include all those who were involved.

In all cases of reward and recognition, the basis must be objective and quantified. This expands the environment of fairness and honesty throughout the organization. It makes and keeps the commitment of the executive and ambassadors to a high-integrity organization apparent. Moreover, it fosters and supports the reality of associate contribution as being the cornerstone of the organization's ability to achieve the dream.

ℰ◉ℰ

Loyalty, Morale, and the Executive Thinking Organization

Like many other supposedly amorphous concepts, morale and loyalty are treated as intangible entities that no individual within the organization can implement or affect. This is not the case. Like trust and the creation of the appropriate environment, consistent demonstration of behaviors supportive of the morale or loyalty outcome will generate the desired result.

Ultimately, through the clear delineation of expectations and commitments across and throughout the organization, and because of the active participation of the associates within their thinking environment, a new and higher level of morale will exist within the organization. This, in concert with the respect and reward given to the associates for their thoughts, actions, and contributions, will lead to a higher level of loyalty than previously existed.

It is the responsibility of the executive and his ambassadors to ensure that the environment, values, and goals that they have established and communicated to the associates are consistently demonstrated and supported. This consistency will lead to the higher morale and existence of loyalty, which are such necessary components for the organization to succeed over the long term.

Neither of these outcomes should be treated lightly. There are direct costs and benefits associated with morale and loyalty. When the morale of the organization is high, its associates are at their most productive. They are satisfied with their work and their work environment. They are engaged in the goals and direction of the enterprise. They see their value to the organization and have that value recognized on a regular basis. They are happy with their work and, as such, are not distracted by thoughts of dissatisfaction. All of this translates to a high quality of work at a high level of productivity.

Loyalty demonstrates its profitability through reduced turnover. Associates satisfied with their jobs remain in those jobs. They believe that the management of the organization supports them and, in return, they demonstrate their support for management and the organization by doing the best job they can. They speak well of the organization both on- and off-site. They are proud of their work and they know that that pride is reflected throughout the organization at all levels.

Increased morale and loyalty are outgrowths of the reciprocal systems embedded within Executive Thinking. The process makes concrete the previously considered amorphous entities and activities that lead to a satisfied and satisfying workplace. In part this is accomplished by the associates themselves through their contributions to the definition, design, and manifestation of their preferred workplace and work environment. The reciprocity comes from the executive and ambassadors' support for the changes that must be made to ensure the achievement of the dream.

Recently, much has been said about the Generation X employees and their views of loyalty. These employees, if what is written is to be believed, have no loyalty to any organization. They come to the organization looking exclusively for what the organization can do for them. They take as much as they can out of it and then, when the organization has fulfilled their needs, they leave it without a backward glance. This is supposedly due to the Generation X belief that organizations have no loyalty to their employees, as demonstrated by the layoffs experienced by their parents. Accordingly, they take their need for instant gratification and their belief that there is no loyalty, and they simply use the organization for their own ends.

In fact, humans are humans. Whether Generation X or the "flower children" of generations past, each generation brings its own concerns to the workplace. Societies change and, as such, the associated life needs change. This does not happen overnight, nor is it unpredictable. But, no matter what the changes, the human need for respect and thoughtfulness remains a constant.

The Generation X pattern of changing jobs that is considered so new and unfamiliar to organizations is, in fact, no different from the pattern women learned in organizations after the advent of the women's movement. In the case of women, because there was rarely a clear-cut career ladder in any one organization, they learned to move every two to three years. This provided them with the promotion opportunities that were lacking on a by-company basis.

Where Generation X employees are considered disloyal, women were considered inconsistent and undedicated to the workplace. In both cases, the assessment was wrong. Then and now, as well as in countless other situations in other times, the actions taken were taken in response to the limitations of the system of that day. They were not a commentary. However, they were a sign of things that would need to change.

In the case of Generation X, indeed for all associates belonging to any generation, the change comes from the advent of Executive Thinking. This process addresses the issues that are confronting the organization and that keep the enterprise from achieving and exceeding its goals. The reason they can be addressed is because it is the associates who are participating in the dialogue and identifying the issues. It is also the associates who are making recommendations and taking actions toward the changes that need to be made.

The organization, however, owes no one group or individual anything more than that group or individual is willing to contribute to the enterprise. Organizations succeed as a result of reciprocity. Associates must contribute to the organization. The organization, in the form of its systems, procedures, environment, and rewards, ad infinitum, must reciprocate by doing everything it can to enable the associates to make the best contributions possible.

The more and greater the associates become involved in Executive Thinking and, in fact, develop as executives in their own right, the more the organization will be able to fulfill their needs. The executive must shift his attention to the needs of the organization. He must be committed to ensuring the ability of everyone within the organization to make the greatest contribution possible. It begins with his ambassadors. It expands to include every associate throughout the enterprise. Ultimately, this makes the issue of Generation X or any other single identifiable group moot. Everybody is engaged. Everybody is involved. And everybody, in working toward the same goals, is rewarded.

This reciprocity is in the executive's and the associates' best interests, as well as in the best interests of the organization. The more that is done toward the achievement of the dream, the more the organization will benefit. These benefits will not be limited to the profitability of the organization. While the organization will accomplish more than it ever has and more than was ever dreamed, those accomplishments will be far outstripped by the human achievements within the organization. By committing to the dream, everyone in the organization gains the opportunity to achieve an even greater humanity in his own as well as in his associates' lives.

E X E C U T I V E   T H O U G H T S

The executive must make it abundantly and consistently clear that only the best will be expected and accepted from everyone. She must then, working with her ambassadors on an ongoing basis throughout the process, ensure that everything possible within the organization is being done to support the associates.

The raising of organizational expectations must be insinuated into the organization. It begins by discussing what is already known to the associates. It progresses by examining that which was considered impossible. It becomes integrated by regular and rational discussion of what had previously been unimaginable.

The organization owes no one group or individual anything more than that group or individual is willing to contribute to the enterprise. Organizations succeed as a result of reciprocity. Associates must contribute to the organization. The organization must reciprocate by doing everything it can to enable the associates to make the best contributions possible.

CHAPTER 9

INTEGRATION

THE SINGLE MOST CHALLENGING POINT IN the process for the executive is when full-scale implementation begins. As the dream starts to be initiated into the organization, the executive will find herself back where she was when she first established the dream and communicated it to her ambassadors. For her, the organization will be far behind where it should be. The dream should already have manifest itself. For the executive, the waiting is the worst.

The executive must be particularly gentle with herself and with the organization in these earliest stages. She must once again rely on the ground rules that have served her so well up to this point. Now, however, the ground rules have a slightly different meaning and manifestation than they had in the dream development process. They are action and observation oriented rather than purely thinking oriented. They also have a broader-based application than before. While the ground rules had initially applied only to the executive, they now must be applied to the organization as a whole.

Organizational Application of the Ground Rules

The first ground rule is that there are no wrong answers. At the initiation of implementation, this means that the organization is growing into the dream. As such, ambassadors and associates will be testing the dream. They will ask questions to see whether and how it makes sense for them and for their part of the enterprise.

For the executive, this can be a painful part of the process. She has invested so much of herself in the dream and her belief in it, and in what the organization can do, that hearing the comments and seeing what seems a lack of action can be misinterpreted as betrayal by the organization. It can be misconstrued as a lack of support. It is not. It is the normal, expected thinking process that each individual must pursue to establish his own meaning for the dream.

As such, there are no wrong answers. Each individual is working to understand and apply the dream to his own agenda. Further, he is attempting to assess the extent to which the organization and the executive are truly committed to the establishment of the dream and all that that will entail. Much like the process the executive pursued in establishing her dream, she is, in fact, watching her organization adopt and adapt her dream to fulfill its own needs and direction.

Ultimately the body of the organization will see what the executive sees. Until that time, the executive and the ambassadors must give serious attention to the questions asked and comments made. Where associates are misunderstanding or misinterpreting the dream, the executive and ambassadors must provide clarification. Where associates are testing the dream and, more important, the commitment to the dream, the executive and ambassadors must be patient and hold the course.

The second ground rule, suspend disbelief, also takes on a different caste during implementation. In this case, the executive observes her ambassadors and associates struggling to believe that the organization will, in fact, remain committed to this direction. Too much history has passed with too many conflicting directions for the body of the organization to simply accept that this time will be different.

Even more challenging will be the acceptance of the changes in behaviors and expectations that are embedded in Executive Thinking. When the components of trust, the establishment of a community, and the development of an integrated environment are first being observed, there will be expected confusion and skepticism. Modeling new behavior is not easy. The belief by the members of the enterprise that these behaviors will remain consistent is something that can only be proved over time.

And, finally, the greatest challenge for the associates, in particular, will be in accepting that the organization truly is interested in their thoughts. Remember that these thoughts either have not previously been communicated or have been spoken of in complaint form only with colleagues and co-workers. The idea and, ultimately, the belief that the executive is truly interested in the associates' thoughts and that something will happen as a result of that thinking is initially very difficult to accept.

In this case, the executive will not be suspending her disbelief about her and the organization's ability to achieve the dream. Instead, she will be observing the process pursued by the ambassadors and associates as they come to the realization that they, too, must suspend their disbelief and accept that what is now the case will continue to be the case. In effect, as the body of the organization is asking the question, "Am I seeing what I think I'm seeing?" the executive's consistent answer will be, "Yes."

The third ground rule, to monitor behavior, now has a combined focus for the executive. The associates and ambassadors, in their testing process, will be closely observing the executive to ensure her commitment and consistency with regard to her own dream. To that end, the executive will have to monitor her own behavior to ensure that it is in alignment with the behavioral components and dream-related requirements she has conveyed to the organization.

The executive must also closely monitor the behavior of her organization as the initiation and implementation is taking place. She must understand that the organization is experiencing growing pains. Through the communication of the dream and the initiation of Executive Thinking, associates throughout the organization are being asked to adopt a new way of doing business. They are being asked to participate in and take ownership of the enterprise to an extent they have never before encountered. They are being asked questions and having their answers listened to. Even more, they are expected to actively participate in the manifestation of their thoughts into actions and, ultimately, into the achievement of the dream.

This is not an easy transition for the associates or for the ambassadors. Roles will be changing and then changing again. Trust will be built and empowerment enacted. Intolerance for inactivity or intentional disregard will be apparent. The executive will be seeing the organization she has always envisioned. The associates will be seeing an organization the likes of which they have never dreamed before.

The executive must display a certain amount of tolerance and patience for the transition requirements of her organization. She also must understand that no matter how often and in how many ways she communicates the dream, her listeners will always hear something different from what she is saying. This is a function of human communication and cannot be avoided.

To the executive, the dream is very clear. She has thought about it, honed it, discussed it with her ambassadors, and worked with it until she can describe it in glowing and glorious detail. From the executive's perspective, even though she has experienced the challenges encountered during the developmental understanding process with her ambassadors, the dream has always been very clear. In the executive's view, the dream should be understood by all who hear it. As noted before, this will not be the case.

A groundbreaking theory of communication developed in the 1930s has particular application at this point in the process. A model was designed to describe the physical process of telephone usage: one person called another; the other received the call; a message was conveyed through the lines; and the sender and the receiver could provide feedback to one another. Later, it was realized that this was also a model of the ways by which humans give and receive messages—as well as a description of the ways by which those messages go awry.

The premise of the model is simple. There is, on one end, a sender—the person conveying the message. On the other end, there is a receiver—the person to whom the message is being conveyed. In between and connecting the two there is the message—the information that is being conveyed by the sender to the receiver. Messages move in both directions. The sender and receiver change roles depending upon who is speaking and who is listening at any given time during the interaction.

The model also introduced a concept not previously known or thought of in communication research prior to that time. The concept was noise.

In the middle of the message connecting the sender to the receiver is noise. When the model was first designed, the noise was put there to represent the sound of static through the telephone lines that kept the sender and receiver from being able to communicate clearly. As the model was adapted for human communication research, noise took on a completely different meaning. For humans, the noise is the individual interpretation and understanding of what is being communicated. That interpretation and understanding is different for every individual because every individual has his own experiences and his own perceptions. While others might share those experiences and perceptions, they are wholly individual in the ways in which they are interpreted, understood, and applied.

Using this model as a basis for understanding, the executive must realize that what she believes she is so clearly communicating is, in fact, moving through noise before it is received by her hearers. Ambassadors, working ambassadors, and associates all hear the message differently. They see the picture described by the executive differently.

While there will be many similarities in the understanding and interpretation of the picture described to the listeners, there will be many more differences—particularly in the earliest stages. That is why it is so important for the executive to communicate her dream in as many ways as possible as often as possible to her organization. The more she communicates and models the dream, the progressively less noise there will be in the communication process. It is not only a function of the hearers believing what the executive is saying; it is that the more often the dream is communicated, in as many contexts as possible, the more the executive's associates can actually hear the dream for what it is. From that point, they will not only hear it, they will see it, and they will act on it.

For the executive, noise occurs slightly later in the process. The dream has belonged to the executive for a long time. It has meaning and importance to her. As a result, as she hears questions and comments from others about her dream, those messages move not only through the noise of her experience but also through the noise of ownership.

Pragmatically the executive understands that once the dream goes public and moves into implementation it will change form. It has to. As the dream gains breadth, depth, and detail from the associates, it will no longer look exactly like the dream envisioned by the executive — nor should it if it is to be manifest.

The executive cannot be dogmatic about an exclusive manifestation of only her version of the dream. If she is — in effect, if she allows her dogmatism to act as noise and keep her from learning what she needs to know about how to ensure achievement of the dream — the dream will not succeed. The executive must monitor herself as she listens to the thoughts of the ambassadors and associates to ensure that she is reducing her noise level to the greatest possible extent.

Finally, the fourth ground rule, that of separating the dream from the individual, also takes on a different interpretation during implementation. For the associates, particularly in the earliest stages of implementation, the dream will be inextricably bound with the executive. To that point, the dream is not yet theirs. The executive must understand that when she first communicates the dream, she is seen as the keeper of the dream. The organization looks to her to determine the extent to which she is committed. That is part of the testing. For the associates, probably the most important part of that testing is the extent to which the executive visibly ensures that her ambassadors and their working ambassadors consistently and continuously integrate and model the dream.

The associates will be using the ambassadors as a gauge of the executive's commitment. They do this, first, because it is easier to monitor the behavior of more immediate management than that of the executive. Second, they are more greatly and immediately impacted by their ambassadors and working ambassadors than they are by their executive. If the executive is committed, the associates should quickly see a difference in their work environment. As they see those differences, they will begin to join the executive as keepers of the dream.

For the executive, the fourth ground rule also manifests itself as she looks at the ways by which the organization is responding to the initiation and implementation of the dream. In particular during the early stages, the executive must separate the individuals from their interpretation, and possible misinterpretation, of the dream. While she should expect some problems and even possible attempts at sabotage, some of the missteps will be simply that—missteps. There will be no underlying intent to hurt the dream or the organization. There will simply be misunderstandings of the intent, direction, and manifestation of the dream until such time as the dream is truly understood.

The executive will, of course, be vigilant in looking at the progress from the beginning toward the achievement of the dream. As part of that analysis, she will be able to quickly see the missteps that are taken. She will also be able to discern which of those missteps are simple mistakes and which have a more sinister and intentional purpose. For those that are mistakes, she will once again communicate and clarify the dream. For those that have an alternative intent, she will determine the correct and appropriate action and then take that action quickly and cleanly.

It is not necessary for the executive to communicate the ground rules, per se, to the organization as it moves toward implementation. She may have communicated the rules earlier to the ambassadors during the initial discussions of the dream. If that is the case, she may now decide to discuss the organizational implications and application of the ground rules as the process moves forward. If the executive believes that discussing the ground rules will assist the ambassadors in clarifying the process and expectations, then she should do so. Otherwise, and particularly on the broader organizational basis, the thinking, trust, and environmental behaviors that are being manifest will act as the ground and operating rules for the organization. This will lessen the possibility of confusion and ensure a simpler, more elegant line through implementation and toward integration of the process and of the dream.

Implementation Speed and Integration

Executive Thinking, indeed the full manifestation of the dream, will move in fits and starts. Certain parts of the organization will grab onto the dream and move quickly into its implementation. Other parts of the organization will have a more difficult time understanding, accepting, and applying the dream to its operations. These functions will move more slowly into implementation. Eventually, the whole organization will be involved and the process will smooth and even out.

For those portions of the organization that move out most quickly, the executive and ambassador of that area should ensure that the actions being taken are wholly representative of the dream. Certain actions that should and need to be taken will be taken right away. However, the executive and ambassador must remember that the accomplishment of the dream includes the organization's ability to exceed the initial dream and pursue further dreams over time. If the actions taken are taken purely on a task basis and the necessary changes to the environment—most particularly the incorporation of Executive Thinking—are not made, the dream will be only partially realized. In effect, that function will be going through the motions by taking actions it has probably needed to take for a long time. This is not Executive Thinking. This is simple problem solving. Instead, the functions must access and utilize the most that all of the associates have to offer—their thoughts, creativity, and commitment to action.

In contrast, those parts of the organization that take longer to move into implementation and manifestation will probably do a better job of integrating the thinking process into the dream. These functions will be taking their time in determining their part of the dream. They will be involved in the dialogue about the dream and how their particular function fits into that context. They will discuss their jobs and how those jobs are now being performed. They will generate ideas that go beyond the immediate, known recommendations for improvement. Not only will they enact the dream as it has been described, but they will also begin to dream a dream of their own—a dream of their function as they would truly like to see it.

This is not to say that fast is bad and slow is good. For the executive, the hallmark is that thinking is going on. He must be in close contact with his ambassadors to ensure that they see the thinking activities that are to be expected as part of the process. Together, the executive and ambassadors must see that each function is working toward the development of the breadth and depth of the dream—filling in the Technicolor components—and taking action toward those ends.

Eventually the speed and acceptance of the implementation process will smooth out across the organization. As each function begins working toward its own goals and coordinating with its associated functions, the associates will have to accommodate themselves to the greater need. No one function will be able to push another function to move too quickly. Unthinking actions will be identified and stopped before they are taken. The associates will work together, within and across functions, to ensure that they all are realizing the dream. Otherwise, as they will well know, the dream will not be realized at all.

As the speed smoothes out, it will also increase. Where the executive begins the initiation and implementation process frustrated by the apparent slowness of the process, he must quickly adjust to an organization that is designed to move as fast as if not faster than the dream. Associates, as they learn that they will be listened to and allowed to act upon their ideas, will begin generating those ideas at a much quicker pace. Further, as the associates learn that they can work with other functions on shared goals, the ideas and their associated actions become exponentially manifest. It is no longer individuals who are working the dream. It is multiples of those individuals located in every division, department, function, and location of the enterprise. They all see the dream and they are all working toward its achievement. They are on the same side—the side of the organization—and all of their decisions are based on the dream in context and the dance in action.

This is another point of freedom for the executive and his ambassadors. As they see the ways by which the organization is accepting and enacting the dream, they will be able to assess how best to move the dream into its next iteration. They will be looking at external as well as internal factors. They must assess the needs of the marketplace and their organization's current and preferred placement in that marketplace. They balance their knowledge of the external indicators—the first universe—with their greater understanding of how the organization operates — the second universe. They combine the two universes and then direct their attention to the new goals that they identify. As applicable ideas are offered, they incorporate strategic thinking from the associates to further enhance and augment the next dream.

Even before the first dream is fully realized, the executive and ambassadors begin the process of expanding that dream to incorporate the even greater direction for the organization. In that way, everyone's thinking is always engaged, the organization is designed to consistently and continuously build upon its successes, and there is never a moment during which the organization languishes.

ℰ◉ℰ

Problems as a Positive Force

No matter how smoothly planned, no matter how well designed, there will be problems and obstacles encountered during implementation. Executive Thinking represents a deep-seated change in the way the organization does business. The greatest change is the level of responsibility and accountability residing with the ambassadors and associates. For most this will be a change to the good. However, for some this will represent a degree of risk and danger that will make them actively uncomfortable in the enterprise.

In any of these cases and more, some problems should be expected. They should also be treated as gifts to the organization because they represent the best learning opportunities the enterprise can be given.

When things are going well, humans have a tendency not to question. There are no concerted analyses to determine how everything is being done so that it can be replicated. There is no great desire to look at the operation because there seems to be no need to do so. There is a simple, unconscious acceptance that everything is just fine. There is a corollary unconscious belief that now that everything is fine it will stay fine. The executive and associates know that that is not really the case. However, during the good times the operating mode is one of acceptance of good fortune and belief in continuity.

In many ways, problems are the preferred operating mode for the organization. While no one consciously wants them, it is when problems arise that the organization thrives. It is at this point that the enterprise puts its best foot forward and shows just what it can do. The question is, why does this happen only in the bad times? Why doesn't the organization demonstrate the full breadth and depth of its capabilities during the good times as well?

The main reason is because there is seemingly no reason to do so. What is being done is considered adequate and acceptable. It is more than just "If it ain't broke, don't fix it." It is a complacence that is accompanied by a refusal to look too deeply into the operations and a resulting invisibility of the opportunities to excel.

One executive cited an example of how this phenomenon plays out annually in his organization. He explained that his industry follows the "talk is cheap" pattern each year at budget time. The fiscal year comes to an end at just the same time that the industry and the business are most profitable. Every year as the next year's budget is being determined, all of the senior executives meet and talk about all of the new and innovative things they will do the next year. They talk about the changes that need to be made and how they plan to make them. However, as the fiscal year starts coming to its end, everybody knows that the discussed improvements will not be enacted. By the time the budget is approved, the business is doing well, and so, it is argued, there is no reason to do more. As a result, no additional funding for new projects is requested. Then, during the parts of the year when the business is challenged, all of those same executives complain about the things that they need to do but have no money to do—thus eventually leading into the next year's budget discussions and a continuation of the pattern.

The executive must be vigilant in changing the culture of the organization away from one of complacency and actively toward one of challenge and change. The dream is only the start. Prior to Executive Thinking, the organization has accessed the abilities and commitment of its associates only when times are bad. Problems are used as a call to arms, gathering everyone together in fighting the good fight. Up until this point, problems have acted as the rallying cry for the organization.

Unconsciously, problems of any size and scope are treated as if they are good for the organization. They provide the executive and associates an understandable, comparative position from which to view the operation.

They also provide the impetus and motivation to take that analytical look. No one wants the organization to operate in a problematic way. By looking at the problem, the executives and associates can look for solutions. Once they have identified and implemented those solutions, the organization can continue going forward as before—or, preferably, better.

Problems and obstacles are usually and often referred to as "challenges" and "opportunities." Many executives actually say that as a directive to their associates: "There are no problems. There are only challenges and opportunities." Whether they are referred to as problems, obstacles, challenges, or opportunities, they provide the same gift to the organization—they motivate the executive and associates to take an objective look at the enterprise, identify how things are being done, determine a better way, and provide the impetus to make the changes that need to be made.

The greatest challenge for the Executive Thinking organization is to take that problem-to-solution mentality and apply it to all operations all the time. In that way, problems do become gifts. Every obstacle that presents itself is viewed as another opportunity to learn about the organization. The executive and associates must constantly be questioning why things work as they do. Over time, the problems that will be analyzed will no longer be apparent obstacles. Eventually, this questioning process—as well as the process of taking the badness out of the idea of problems and change—will become the operating norm.

In looking at and preparing for the obstacles the enterprise will encounter during implementation, the executive and associates must view these obstacles as learning opportunities. They provide the chance for the organization to know more about itself, to accept and build upon those aspects of its operations that are believed to be in its best interests, and to change those operations that need to be changed. These problems, as with all problems encountered by the organization, provide food for thought and a springboard for new ideas and actions.

Any time a problem is encountered or identified, the executive and associates should begin by determining why this problem occurred. Unless this analysis is pursued from the first, there will be a tendency to move directly to solutions and lose the opportunity to ensure that the problem will not recur. The "why" analysis provides the organization with the understanding of its operations. The solution can be a real solution only if that analysis is pursued and completed.

Granted, if the problem identified is of crisis proportions, then there may be no time for an initial analysis. However, if the executive does not commit to a follow-on analysis, the problems encountered will recur—no matter how satisfying the solution to the immediate circumstance.

This lack of "why" analysis explains why most change and improvement initiatives do not work over the long term. In contrast to Executive Thinking, most change efforts are designed exclusively as problem-solving mechanisms. There is a tendency to focus on the metaphorical low-hanging fruits because they are the easiest and most visible changes to be made. These changes do not challenge the fundamentals of the organization. They simply address problems that everyone knows need to be solved.

The "why" analysis challenges the fundamentals of the organization. The executive and associates deeply question how the situation has come to pass. They further analyze how the operation has been supporting that particular state of affairs. There is a determination of how the situation as it exists assists some areas of the enterprise while hurting others. Prior to making any changes, assessments are made to ensure that the changes will not hurt any part of the organization while they are helping the area affected by the problem itself.

Because this is now an organization that works in the white space, associates understand that there is a commitment to something more than just their function or the solution to their problem. "Their" problem is no longer just theirs. It is a situation confronting the organization that is used, first and foremost, to learn how to avoid other such situations in the future. The problem is a gift of learning and is to be used as such.

The human dynamic problems that the organization encounters in Executive Thinking should be treated in exactly the same way. Before decisions are made about what to do about a particular circumstance or individual, the executive and ambassadors must assess why this situation has come to pass. They must work with the individual to determine the intent of the actions. This will assist the executive and ambassadors in determining the best actions to take to support both the enterprise and the individuals who make up the enterprise.

On Tolerance

The Executive Thinking organization is both a more tolerant and a more intolerant organization than the norm. The tolerance in the organization demonstrates itself particularly in the thinking process. Initial thinking tends to be safe thinking. Ambassadors and associates work from what is known rather than delve into arenas that are new to them. As they begin feeling safer in the process, their thinking begins to expand. Suddenly it is no longer enough to look at what is. They begin to look at what might be.

This type of creative, innovative thinking leads to new products, services, and markets. It removes the previously believed limitations on the organization and creates a limitless entity that operates wholly from the basis of opportunity. There is nothing the organization cannot do should it so decide. This is more than creative thinking. This is off-the-wall thinking. Ideas that were previously considered impossible are now actively assessed for their possibilities. Discussion that would never have been tolerated in the past becomes the norm of the present.

It is at this point that the dream stops being a goal and starts becoming a jumping-off point for the organization. Where at the beginning of the process the dream seemed to many an impossible goal, manifestation toward the dream becomes so commonplace that the dream is no longer enough. It is the ideas attached to this level of thinking that the executive looks for from her organization and that she will incorporate to as great an extent as possible into the next levels and iterations of the dream.

It is also the dream that makes the organization an intolerant enterprise. As previously discussed, the organization neither can nor will tolerate intentional inaction or misdirection against the dream. This intolerance is crucial for the success of the organization.

Prior to the inception and communication of the dream, there were no real or concrete guidelines to show the associates exactly what the organization was working toward or stood for. The dream is not only a dream of product and profit, it is also a dream of operations and environment. As such, it is a dream that everyone can understand and from which they benefit. As a guideline, the dream also acts as an informal set of rules and expectations, both hierarchically and within levels and functions.

Ambassadors and associates must assess the extent to which their actions and the actions of their colleagues and co-workers work toward the achievement of the dream. There can be no tolerance for associates, at any level, who do not adopt the dream as their goal and their operating guideline. There is no time for the organization to languish while trying to reverse an associate's attitude toward the dream. If the associate is not convinced that the dream is for him—or at least that he can actively and positively work toward its achievement whether he adopts it or not—and his behavior is not in support of the dream, he should leave. The organization is no longer the right place for him to be.

Organizations neither can be nor have the time to be soft. Tolerance within the organization resulted from a lack of understanding of exactly what was going on and why. Executive Thinking provides that necessary level of understanding. There is no longer any guessing attached to how the organization operates. The expectations and commitments are detailed, communicated, and modeled. The organization is tracking and monitoring its performance. What was previously considered surprising is now considered predictable. The only question to be answered is whether what is now predictable is acceptable and preferred. If so, continue. If not, change.

As a simple and elegant operation, the Executive Thinking organization is built on the system of combined tolerance and intolerance. Support for the organization is tolerated in any and all forms. It is part of the alignment—that simple and elegant line. Lack of support for the organization—in any form—is not tolerated and actions are taken.

This is not inhumane. In fact, it provides the greatest support to those who are working toward the goals of the organization. Rather than inordinate amounts of time being spent supporting and assisting the problematic few, the enterprise is designed to support and assist the supportive many. The investment of time and energy is simply being made where there will be the greatest return. It is a business decision with very humane overtones and outcomes.

ㄷⓞ੭

Preparing the Working Ambassadors for Executive Thinking

One of the most common potential problems associated with Executive Thinking is the extent to which the working ambassadors are or are not prepared for their role. The executive is so fully conversant with and committed to the dream that for him it is already real. For the ambassadors the dream is new, but because they have a part in the dream's development before the executive takes it public, they, too, become owners of the dream from the early stages. The working ambassadors must be fully prepared for their role as the most immediate and frequent communicators and models of the dream.

As the ambassadors become conversant with the dream—even before it is taken public by the executive—they will find themselves insinuating the dream into their discussions with their immediate reports, the working ambassadors. This is for the good. This begins preparing the working ambassadors for what they have yet to hear and to manage as the organization embraces the dream.

Staff meetings begin to take on the characteristics of the dialogue. Discussion and positive discourse occur. The working ambassadors are provided with the same opportunities to disagree and express concern as the ambassadors were given by the executive in the initial discussions of the dream.

The working ambassadors are not necessarily aware that they are participating in a developmental process. Instead, they are experiencing the trust behaviors modeled by their ambassadors. They are being asked questions that they have not previously been asked. To the extent appropriate, aspects of the dream are being insinuated into the discussions as an assessment of obstacles to be approached, but also as a means of preparing the working ambassadors for their changing role in the organization.

For without a doubt, it will be the working ambassadors who will be the most consistent and operational speakers of the dream throughout the organization. It is they who will bring the same types of dialogue that they have experienced and continue to experience to their functional areas. It will be the working ambassadors who most visibly assist the associates in adapting to their new role.

By the time the executive publicly addresses the dream and the organization moves toward full engagement, the working ambassadors have begun becoming Executive Thinkers in their own right. They have raised questions and, most likely, have already made or at least thought of changes to their part of the organization. They are prepared for and unknowingly versed in the dream and their part in its achievement and success.

They understand the dialogue process because they have engaged in dialogue with their ambassadors. They have become comfortable with the concept and behaviors associated with positive disagreement. They understand that they will not, nor should they, see each and every situation in the same way as everybody else. It is the differences that bring great value, breadth, and depth to the dream.

As the dream is introduced to and becomes a part of the organization, they understand that the differences they identify are, in fact, a demonstration of their commitment to the organization and to the executive's dream. They know that the more they contribute to the achievement of the dream, the more satisfaction and success they will incur.

They are used to the multiple levels of Executive Thinking: as chief executive, chief financial, and chief operating officers. They know that the more knowledge and skill they bring to their own thinking processes, the more they can and will contribute to the organization. They think like executives, and they are treated like executives.

The trust model is one with which they are familiar and that they practice on a regular basis. They no longer speak or think of trust lost. Instead, their focus is on the behaviors necessary to regain and rebuild trust throughout the organization. Further, they concentrate on the long-term maintenance of that trust. They have begun actively working in the white space and are comfortable introducing their associates to those relationships and contacts.

The ambassadors must continue to work with the working ambassadors to ensure that the dream is safe in their hands and in the ways in which they operationally extend the dream to the associates of the organization. The working ambassadors must be as well versed in the dream as the executive and his ambassadors. There must be alignment and continuity throughout the management ranks to ensure that that alignment will extend to all of the associates throughout the enterprise.

ॐ

The Hallmarks of Integration

For the executive and ambassadors, there will be certain phenomena that they will observe during the progress from initiation to integration. These phenomena will be somewhat unnoticeable at first. Over time and in retrospect, they, along with the behavioral factors already described, will be understood as the hallmarks of integration.

First and foremost there is information movement. Information moves as and where needed. Rather than necessary information being treated as a commodity to be protected as a power-growing device, it is shared openly to ensure that everyone knows what she needs to know when she needs to know it.

The information moves in less formalized ways than before. Rather than waiting for formalized times or using formalized mechanisms, the associates work in the white space. Their contact and relationships ensure that the information is moved in the most efficient manner. Also, because all information is used for the greater good, the sender ensures that the information to be conveyed is of the highest integrity possible. This is not a matter of moving rumors or innuendo around the enterprise. It is an intentional movement of necessary information to ensure the greatest outcomes possible.

Decisions are not only made based on that information, making them the best-informed decisions possible, they are also made using the axiom "think globally, act locally." At all levels of the organization, decisions are made on the basis of the interactive effects throughout the organization. The associates understand that the functions of the enterprise are bound together as one. As such, they know that any actions taken in one area of the organization will affect the rest of the organization in some way.

Decisions are made using the dream as the context. Actions taken are assessed both while in progress and after the fact to determine whether all factors were adequately considered. Analyzing and applying lessons learned becomes an operating norm for the organization, both for those decisions that worked and for those decisions that did not work as expected.

Where something has gone wrong, rather than the organization languishing in or blaming anyone for that misdirection, trust is regenerated. The trust components are consistently enacted so that there is no breach in that process. Further, if an associate chooses the role of the victim, the balance of the associates and the working ambassador work with that person to determine whether the role is by accident or with intent. For those associates who fall into the role by accident, they are supported by their co-workers and assisted in their move back into the mainstream. For those who choose the role of victim with intent and also choose to maintain that intent, they are identified and their ambassador works with them to move out of that role, out of the function or, ultimately and if necessary, out of the organization.

The speed of the organization increases. Decisions are made in less time. There is a shorter time period between decisions being made and associated actions being taken. The organization is more flexible and adapts to changes in direction with greater ease and at a higher speed. When those changes occur, the necessary actions are integrated into the various operations faster and better than before.

The only surprises in the organization are surprises on the upside. The organization becomes a fluid, well-designed, and well-tooled machine. It operates exactly as it must and should. There are no longer concerns about an unexpected inability to meet goals or deadlines. Those goals and deadlines are met and often exceeded. The questions of the organization no longer focus on "Why didn't we?" or "Why weren't we able to?" Instead, their focus is, "Now that we have done this much, how much farther do you think we can go?" To that question, the answer is always, "Let's find out."

The thinking process across the organization becomes one of strategy. Although the associates continue to live in a tactical, operational world, they think about that world in a strategic manner. They question what the outcomes would be if they were to make certain changes. They take those changes, apply them to the dream, and then recommend even further changes that might be made. While the changes themselves might be tactical, the intent and outcome feed into the strategy of the organization.

Thinking is concrete. Within the context of the dream, every associate becomes a pragmatic dreamer. He becomes an executive. In discussion, whether with the executive, the ambassadors, or other associates, every associate is action oriented and determined. He knows what needs to be done, and he is relentless in achieving that goal. Without being asked, he offers his thoughts as chief executive, chief operating, and chief financial officers. He asks for information to factor into his thinking before he moves off in an unknown direction. Eventually, he also makes it clear that he no longer needs the immediate guidance that was offered at the initiation of the dream. Now, he is looking for and expecting a higher level of thinking from the executive and her ambassadors. He is looking for what comes next.

For the executive, Executive Thinking provides the greatest learning opportunities of all. Throughout her career she has questioned why certain things have not come to pass. She has wondered why some things that she hoped never to see repeated somehow always recurred. She has always had her vision. What she has not had is the ability to understand why that vision has not fully and completely come to pass.

Throughout Executive Thinking, the answers to these and many more questions will become apparent. The executive will learn why the organization has not achieved its goals in the past and what needs to change so that the organization not only achieves but exceeds its goals on a regular basis. Those things that she never wants to see happen again will not. And, most important, through her own actions and subsequently the actions of all of her associates, she will learn how to turn her vision into a reality that is shared by everyone. She will, in fact, learn that dreams can and do come true.

EXECUTIVE THOUGHTS

The executive must be in close contact with her ambassadors to ensure that they see the thinking activities that are to be expected as part of the process. Together, the executive and her ambassadors must see that each function is working toward the development of the breadth and depth of the dream—filling in the Technicolor components—and taking action toward those ends.

Whether referred to as problems, obstacles, challenges, or opportunities, they provide the same gift to the organization—they motivate the executive and associates to take an objective look at the enterprise, identify how things are being done, determine a better way, and provide the impetus to make the changes that need to be made.

Where at the beginning of the process the dream seemed to many an impossible goal, manifestation toward the dream becomes so commonplace that the dream is no longer enough. It is the ideas attached to this level of thinking that the executive looks for from his organization and that he will incorporate to as great an extent as possible into the next levels and iterations of the dream.

238

Epilogue

One of the skills that most executives don't have is the skill to fully engage in and celebrate their successes. For the executive, the success of today is the result of decisions made long ago. By this time, she is actively involved in the decisions that will affect the organization in the months and years to come. While she has built an organization that has learned to reward and recognize, she has not learned to celebrate her own achievements. For the executive the question is always, What is next? What more can and should we do?

Michael Eisner, Chairman and Chief Executive Officer of the Disney Corporation, gave a pertinent example of this phenomenon during an interview. He was asked how he had felt when the Broadway stage production of *The Lion King* won its Tony Awards. The interviewer spoke of the elation Eisner must have experienced from such an exciting event.

Eisner's response was both typical and descriptive of how executives react to the success of the moment. He explained that while he was very happy about the awards the show won, he had already been actively involved in so many other projects that, other than his satisfaction, he gave the awards little thought. By the time the awards were won, he was making decisions about projects yet to be and years in advance. His attention and excitement were focused on those future activities.

Clearly, it was not that Eisner was not pleased with the awards. He was. However, by the time the awards were conferred, he had already moved on. His focus, the expected focus of an executive, was on the future. Because that production was well in hand and did not need his attention or intervention, he was free to move on to the next project, the next goal, the next decision that needed to be made.

This is an arena in which executives need to learn a new skill set. The executive should allow herself to enjoy the fruits of her labors. Had it not been for her dream, direction, and skill, the organization would not have achieved what it set out to do. Further, had she not created an environment in which everyone could expand and then bask in their thinking, actions, and successes, the dream would not have been realized.

The executive must learn to celebrate. She must allow herself to take a moment to live in the moment. She must learn to join her associates as they celebrate their successes. This not only allows the associates to feel a greater connection to the executive, it also and more importantly allows the executive to bask in her own successes, even if only for a moment.

It is not that by celebrating the executive lessens the importance of the future-oriented decisions that need to be made. In fact, it gives them greater importance. By celebrating successes as they occur, the executive allows herself to see her own value to the organization and to her industry. She gives herself a greater perspective on her contributions to the organization. She is not just the keeper of the dream or the maker of future successes. She, too, is a human who greatly contributes to the enterprise through her belief in herself and in the ability of her organization to achieve and exceed her dream.

ℰℴℛ

Executive Thinking and the Executive Legacy

Once Executive Thinking is well and truly begun, the executive must turn his attention to the next dream. He must dream about not only what he wants the organization to accomplish but what the organization will and must be long after he is gone. It is this legacy that will be accomplished because of Executive Thinking.

Long after the executive has left his position, Executive Thinking will still exist within the enterprise.

It might change form or take on different dimensions as new executives, ambassadors, and associates are brought into the organization. However, that will not take away from all that the executive achieved.

The dream, of course, will already have served the organization well. It will have placed the organization into a position whereby it can continue with its current projects, expand into new markets, and take on completely new products and services. The dream, even after it has long been surpassed, will remain the basis upon which the organization in this newest and better iteration has been built.

Executive Thinking, however, is the greatest legacy that the executive can leave the enterprise. Through his commitment and actions he will have taught the organization how to dream. Associates at all levels will have learned skills and accessed talents they had never before been asked to utilize as part of the organization. Thinking will have become a norm. Each individual will expect not only to contribute her thoughts but to have those thoughts recognized and responded to by her colleagues and co-workers.

The organization and all of its operations will now be operating in the executive's image as he wants that image to be. Each individual will be decisive and action oriented. Each associate will participate in the dream as well as dream her own dream. There will be no languishing because there will be no room for languishing. Every associate at every level will be an executive in her own right. There can be no greater legacy left to the organization and its associates by the executive.

And so it continues. The executive has established his dream for the organization and that dream is being manifest. He provided the opportunity and the direction for the ambassadors and associates to do more and to be more—both for themselves and for the organization—and so they have become. The product, service, and profit expectations and goals are being met and exceeded. The organization is everything the executive could have ever wanted.

But how did it get there? What was it that really happened that was fundamentally different from what had gone on before? What was the key?

The key is in the humanity and respect that the executive has brought to his organization. He has developed an environment that treats people as people—thinking, sentient beings who are always capable of more. He has created an organization, beginning with the way that he has allowed himself to dream, designed to make the most of what those people have to offer and to get the most in return. He has ensured that there is recognition and reward for their contributions. He has engaged his associates at all levels in his dream and challenged and supported them in making that dream come true. He has given of himself in the form of the dream and provided an opportunity for his associates—colleagues and co-workers all—to see and know themselves as integral to his, the dream's, the organization's, and ultimately their own success.

Organizations are not just profit and loss, earnings, and market share. Organizations can exist only because of the people who make up the enterprise. It is their commitment and contributions that make the organization thrive. But, more than anything, it is the executive and his ability to dream and to gain and maintain the trust and belief of his associates in that dream that truly creates the organization of his dreams.

Acknowledgments

No book is ever written by the author alone. In this case, the book could not have existed had it not been for the clients, and particularly the executives, with whom I have worked. Their generosity in sharing their thinking, dreams, and experiences has helped make this book all that it is.

There are certain executives who deserve particular attention. These begin with Mr. Donald E. Antenore of Tropicana Products. It was because of Don that I first learned that executives have dreams—pragmatists though they are—and he generously shared his dream with me.

Ms. Eleanor Brewer of the St. Joseph Health System taught me what it means to be an organizational hero. Her commitment to excellence and innovation creates an environment that allows everyone with whom she comes into contact to excel beyond anything seen before.

Dr. Marlene Coleman of the Cooperative of American Physicians, too, must be thanked for her insight and support. Marlene brings a higher level of thinking to everything she does. She has been and remains both a friend and a role model.

Mr. Harry Karsten of The Karsten Company taught me about the strength and perseverance that every executive brings to his job. He also taught me about the tenacity of the dream—no matter what the obstacles or the delays.

Simply citing these executives seems unfair given the invaluable insight and guidance I have received from so many in the preparation of this manuscript and in my own development. In particular I extend my appreciation to Mr. Tim Carda of Tustin Hospital, Mr. Michael Dillon of the United Parcel Service, Mr. Richard R. Douglas of the Beverly Hills Unified School District, Mr. Gary Dysart of Psomas Associates, The Honorable William Huss, Los Angeles County Superior Court Judge, retired, Captain Bernard Janov, United States Navy, retired, Mr. Scott Karsten of Karsten Homes, Mr. Wayne Kimball of Comdata Corporation, Mr. John Pointer of the Internal Revenue Service, Mr. David Preimesberger of CAP•MPT, Messrs. Frank Reed and Jeffrey Napper and Ms. Artie Watson and Nancy Bloh of the Long Beach Schools Federal Credit Union, Dr. Brenda Reis of Allergan Pharmaceuticals, Mr. Leon Rizio of Grant

Thornton, Ms. Bobbie Sablan of the Immigration and Naturalization Service, Messrs. Ed Schneider, Wilfried Pabst and Randy Gilbert of Triton Container International, Mr. H. Lynn Stafford of Legacy Marketing Group, and Captain Terry Ulaszewski, United States Navy, retired. This list is by no means comprehensive. For all those whom I have missed, please accept my thanks.

I extend my great appreciation and respect to my editors, Ms. Melinda Adams Merino and Ms. Jill Anderson-Wilson, of Davies-Black Publishing. Their insight into and understanding of what I wished to convey in combination with their excellent editorial skills helped make this book what it is.

Ms. Laura Simonds and the associates at Davies-Black have my thanks and appreciation for all their support. I also extend my appreciation to my agent, Ms. Laurie Harper of the Sebastian Agency, for her guidance, support, and patience.

My love and appreciation go to my brothers, David and Sam. Throughout this process they have given me great insight and support. In particular, I extend my appreciation to David for his perspective and understanding of self-respect as well as organizational respect and trust.

And, finally, my thanks and love go to my teacher and mentor, Mr. George Conley. Over the years my work with George and his generosity of spirit have opened up vistas to me that I never knew existed. If there is any one person from whom I have learned that not only are dreams limitless, but so, too, is our ability to achieve those dreams, it is George.